To Al,
Warrior of the [illegible].
best wishes,
Gill Coombes

THE TREMBLING WARRIOR

'Thoughtful and important advice for anyone wanting to stand up and do something meaningful for what they believe in... heartfelt language and a lovely turn of phrase make this book a pleasure to read.'
HOWARD BOORMAN Novelist, activist, facilitator, coach

'Do you feel you would like to make a difference in the world, but become immobilised by doubt? Do you step into situations and then struggle to cope with resistance and challenge? This book shows you are not alone, explaining why this happens and how to deal with it. Recommended for all 'sensitive idealists'.
JEAN BOULTON Author of *Embracing Complexity*

'Good advice about listening to your inner voice and doing what's right for you... fresh perspectives on an important and under-researched dimension of political activism."
DAVID MCQUEEN Activist, lecturer in media and politics

ALSO BY GILL COOMBS

HEARING OUR CALLING: REVISIONING WORK AND THE WORKPLACE

'An insightful treatise guiding us towards happier, more purposeful lives.'
SIMON ROBINSON, co-author, *Holonomics*

'An important and valuable contribution to the work of re-visioning how we want to experience our western societies.'
GLENN EDNEY, author, *The Ocean is Alive*

THE GAME: LIFE VS THE DARK POWERS

'Original, exciting, and deeply refreshing.'
MAC MACARTNEY, author, *Finding Earth, Finding Soul*

'Radical, searching, provocative, well-written, and deeply insightful.'
MALCOLM PARLETT, author, *Future Sense*

THE TREMBLING WARRIOR

A Guide for the Reluctant Activist

GILL COOMBS

Cover picture: Valmaz

Author picture: Peter Harrisson

independently published

First printing: May 2019. ISBN: 9781798036150

This book is dedicated to everyone

striving to protect Life

each in their own way

on this fragile and beautiful world.

CONTENTS

GRATITUDE

Producing this book was a nourishing collaboration with many other Trembling Warriors, as well as activists, artists, therapists, writers, teachers, and dreamers of all kinds. Their rich and diverse stories, reflections, advice, poems, dreams and prayers arrived in a gentle life-bringing trickle: each time I raised my head from weaving someone's piece into the whole, another would appear, creating a blessed flow of thoughtful, honest and inspiring words.

Grateful thanks for conversation, inspiration and more to Adam Dadeby, Anna Lunk, Antonia Murphy, Barry Cohen, Carlos Glover, Emma Kidd, Esme North, Gary Lam, Hamish Clueard, Helle Cook, Helen Allman, Jim Borritt, Jim Jasonek, Juliet Gellatly, Kara Moses, Klara Papp, Larch Maxey, Leeann Kirchner, Liz Clayton-Smith, Mothiur Rahman, Muriel Lewington, Natalie Baker, Ned Hetherington, Paul Hoggett, Rachel Fleming, Rebecca Page-Tickell, Sarah McQueen, Sharon Brown, Stephanie Meakin, Yann Rebour, all the Canaries, and certain other courageous, anonymous souls.

Huge gratitude to those who read and commented so very helpfully on the final text, or portions of it: whether addressing content, style, or some priceless typos: David McQueen, Howard Boorman, Jean Boulton, Glenn Edney, Mothiur Rahman, and Peter Harrisson.

Several people were particularly figural during the writing of this book, and I'm deeply appreciative: Anne Newing for a priceless journey of friendship, and for her wisdom, insight and groundedness in many engaging hours of nattering about Trembling Warriorship. David Blowers for unexpected and providential encouragement, almost limitless patience, and intelligent, stretching, and insightful comments on sections as they emerged. Dee Cunnison, friend and sustainability exemplar, for her talent as broker of information and connections, and for sending a steady stream of events, links and contacts my way. Glenn Edney for unconditional, nourishing friendship, and for cheering me on at both the start and finish; Janey Pares-Edney for energy, love and laughter; and for sticking it out so long; and to both for their loving dedication to Life. Judy Allen for her patient, thoughtful and gracious expertise regarding personality type. Juuso Jokiniemi for inspiring conversations and energising enthusiasm, for contributing his eco-dharma perspective, and for shining his loving kindness around the world. Paula Hermes for her generous sharing, and her courage, honesty, humility, eloquence, and passion: a true, legendary Trembling Warrior who returns again and again to the front line, with radiant beauty shining through her pain for the world. And as always to Peter, whose depths and clarity take me by surprise again and again.

My respect and honour to the mountains, forests and lakes of Telemark, Norway; Shaptor Woods, a pond reflecting several alders, a stunted but thriving oak on a Dartmoor-facing hilltop, a stand of poplars, and a raucous, tantalisingly nomadic flock of jackdaws and rooks.

FOREWORD

There have been many times in history when brave people have stood and turned to face a foe of unimaginable strength and felt wholly under-resourced, under-prepared, and very frightened. Such stories are the stuff of legends and serve us questions that challenge, inspire and terrify. What would I do if I was in the same situation? The question hangs in the wind, impossible to answer - until the time comes. At this point a stillness descends and the gods hold their breath, watch and wait. There is no time in human history that matches the perfect storm that even now crashes on the shoreline of our collective hopes and aspirations for a better world. Were this to be the malign fist of some external power it would be bad enough, but for us to so carelessly disregard the ecosystems that feed and clothe those we say we love, suggests a species that is questioning its own right to a seat at life's table - a species that is considering retirement. This question also hangs in the wind, unanswered for the time being.

It is well known that we often don't fully realise the value of something or someone until the very real possibility of loss casts a long shadow, and threatens the departure of that to which we have previously given scant regard. I am hopeful that as the impending logical outcome of our actions looms close, we may come to realise the depth of our love of life and the privileges that have been heaped upon us, before they are lost forever. Many of us see things rather differently when what we have taken for granted is no longer available. It would be better to consider these things before the gates slam shut, and herein lies an opportunity that swiftly grasped may yet see us lurch from cleverness to wisdom.

It is generally accepted that what we so inadequately refer to as climate change is the biggest single threat to human existence, not to mention the countless other species and habitats that will also be massively, and in many cases, fatefully, impacted. I do not hold this to be true. The greatest threat facing humanity is our passive acquiescence and steadfast addiction to staying with what we know, even should it lead us to the cliff edge. Millions of intelligent, kind, and well-intentioned people are gathered as spectators to the soap opera that we have co-scripted: the institutionalised, conformist connivance of those who believe themselves chained, even when it has always only been the entrancement of a pied piper melody that holds us captive. Trained and enslaved to a story that serves the few and harms the many, we have almost forgotten that the edifice of our belief systems is, and always was, illusory. Everything is available to us were we only to reach out, learn to love again, and take responsibility for our own future and that of our children, grandchildren, and other-than-human relatives.

Courage is not the prerogative of those who feel no fear. It belongs to those who feel fear and yet, nonetheless, turn towards it. It is to us, the multitudes of people who feel fear, that Gill Coombs builds a bridge and invites us to cross. I am one such person. Loving the wild places of mountain, forest and sea, I inveigled myself to the opinion that I could best serve the Earth by remaining hidden from view, quietly tilling a small patch of soil. In itself this choice was entirely valid – were it not for the fact that unconsciously I was blocking my ears, closing my eyes, and hiding from a destiny that waited patiently at my doorstep, persistently ringing the doorbell.

We are not all moved by the same things. For some of us it's all about people, for others it's ideas; for some it's nature, and for many of us it's a combination of these and other things. It doesn't matter: they are all parts of the same extraordinary phenomenon we call life. Turn the pages of this loving, inquisitive, and gentle book. Feel the tenderness, empathy, and quiet warriorship that inhabits each chapter, gather an armful of ideas and retire into the changing room, and one by one try them on. Then draw aside the curtain and resplendent in your new, exquisitely hand-crafted gown, stride out and take your place. You will find a family of friends waiting to welcome you. While there will always be tests and challenges, you are more likely to give credence to the deep satisfaction of knowing that when the time came you stepped forward and took your place.

There is no peace in simply ignoring the door-bell.

Mac Macartney
26th April 2019

INTRODUCTION

1973. We've just visited a dark, silent museum and are ecstatic to be free: out in a sun-dappled forest, vividly alive with song birds, the music of fern-bedecked waterfalls, and that uniquely Welsh tang of sheep and peat. The twisting path suddenly rises more steeply between rocks, and my nine-year-old legs begin to tire. My brother Martin hauls me onto his back, and climbs. I keep sliding down and scrabbling back up, and we're giggling. He crests a boulder, and stops abruptly - and so does his laughter. Looking over his shoulder, I discover why.

Below us, stretching away beyond a sagging barbed wire fence, the forest has been gouged out: an incongruous gash in the land too vast for comprehension after the intricate, richly-populated woodland. Naked and despoiled, the crater gapes like a crusted wound. Huge roaring yellow vehicles, with flashing lights and tyres taller than our father, throw up black dust as they drag out loads of slate blasted from the open quarry.

Martin and I look at one another in silent horror, no words needed to share our shock at the damage to the Eden we've only just fallen in love with. It feels worse than mindless: it feels aggressive, and although I may not know the word, exploitative. We turn away and descend, subdued, back down through a living dream that now feels threatened and vulnerable. In the trees all around us, the birds still are exuberantly singing.

Later, I speak to my father through furious tears for the forest. What can I do to stop this destruction? I feel so small, so ineffectual. He's sympathetic to my anguish, but explains with gentle logic that if we want roads - so we can go on holiday to Wales, for example - we need quarries. And he knows: he's a highway engineer. I cry bitterly that I will never travel on roads again. Three days later I rationalise my vow out of existence, so that I can go home. But from that day, I know the way humans inhabit the world is *wrong*. For many years I can't express this sense of knowing, never hearing anyone else speak my heart.

Today, in my work of helping people with questions of identity, purpose and personal transition, I engage most days with the challenges and dreams of people seeking to serve the greater good in some way. It's a source of pleasure, poignancy, often fun, and sometimes love, to witness and support their journeys. But at the heart of all my endeavours remains my eternal sweetheart: our living planet that scientist James Lovelock has named Gaia, in all her beauty, complexity, and diversity. Learning that my first and best love is in grave danger has impelled me to step out of my comfort and into vulnerability, in my various attempts to protect her. My own experience of (sometimes reluctant) activism weaves through this book, alongside the stories of others moved to defend what they care most about.

This book was dreamed into being from the storehouse of my own psyche, deeply rooted in the natural world. That is its source. But when I invited stories from reluctant activists, people I somehow hadn't expected got in touch. Some you'll find in these pages; I also heard about parents fighting for their dyslexic child, a grandmother challenging the laws around social care, and a sensitive, intelligent man still experiencing repercussions from a crime he committed forty years ago: yearning to challenge the judiciary system, but afraid of his past being seen and judged harshly. All are in service to some aspect of Life.

James, a young man I was once mentoring, told me during a conversation about finding work that's good for the world, "I can see where you're coming from, but then you love the planet."

That threw me for a moment. "Are you saying you don't?"

James, a sensitive young man who'd spent a lot of time outside as a boy, answered, "Well, of course I enjoy nice scenery." His response (which was, of course, far from unusual) encapsulated for me the desperately sad, centuries-long human error of perceiving nature as there primarily for our use and entertainment. James didn't need to care about the planet, or take any responsibility for its wellbeing, because he wasn't an 'environmentalist'. And as for love...

The environment suggests something detached and abstract: something that's 'out there', and largely optional. *Gaia*, though, is that precious, tactile, life-abundant entity of which humans are merely a small part: she provides for all our needs, and she is our home. All her life forms deserve heartfelt respect as beings in their own right with long evolutionary histories, complex social lives, endlessly diverse ways of birthing, and bindingly interwoven reciprocal relationships. Damage one aspect of the planetary ecosystem, and you endanger the whole. Today, 'environmentalism' can no longer be seen as a hobby. 'Save the Whale' doesn't seem like such an amusing jibe as it did in the materialistic eighties, now that dead whales regularly wash up on the beach with bellies full of plastic – bringing it home to us. Care for the planet affects us all, as centuries of cumulative thoughtlessness and lack of respect begin to throw it into chaos.

As the chaos becomes increasingly apparent, developed society is being riven in two. There are several ways the split is manifesting: the political left and right; freedom and control; 'stuff' and spirituality; 'mainstream' (which for our purposes means the establishment, consumer culture, individualism, a battle with nature, profit above all) and 'alternative' (community, localism, respect, wellbeing, Life before profit). In Norway, billions of barrels of oil lie under the pristine Lofoten Islands. The political left is split about whether to support oil workers, or leave this fossil fuel where it belongs. In the UK, sand martins' nests are netted over as Norfolk Council tries to decide between protecting endangered birds, or a nearby gas terminal. The human story is dis-integrating; maybe that needs to happen before it can dissolve into reintegration. Some of us choose consciously: others simply ally ourselves to a lifestyle through our actions. Lean one way, you're a snowflake. Lean the other way, you're a Nazi. Of course, it's not such a clean split on the ground, or even within each of us. All these 'sides' don't map exactly on to each other: sociologists could spend years debating the nuances. But viewed from a perspective of distance, the rift is as clear as the Grand Canyon from space.

I wrote about the widening of the rift, and the heightening tension between either side of it, in my last book: *The Game: Life vs The Dark Powers*. Writing for practical people who just want to know what to do, I presented a scenario in which daily actions score for either Life or the Dark Powers – whether we choose to play or not. Since it was published in 2016, the polarisation has become overt: showing up in politics, the tweets of public figures, on the news, and in the rise of activist groups of all types. As we become more aware, ordinary people are finding we must choose: how and where we shop; what products we use in the house; who or what we prioritise when we garden; how, and how often we travel; who we bank with; the work we choose to do, the online groups we belong to.

The last few years have also brought a seismic shift in eco-awareness. The powerful Blue Planet exposé of plastics in the ocean caught the public's attention, which in turn instigated commercial policy changes. It's a dream coming true for 'environmentalists', but perhaps surprising – and for some, frustrating – that David Attenborough waited until his seventh decade of broadcasting to speak out about plastics and climate change. Indeed, he's spoken of his regret at holding back for so many years from talking in wildlife documentaries about the frightening environmental degradation he'd witnessed. Maybe 2017 was the right time: it became possible for Attenborough to speak into a growing awareness due to the work of many local campaigns such as *A Plastic Planet*, which had by then achieved plastic-free supermarket aisles in some countries. Had he spoken earlier, to a public manipulated into blocking its ears, he may have alienated viewers. Had he challenged the neoliberal economic model before becoming such an icon, the BBC may have whisked away his platform. We can never know what would have happened...

Today, in 2019, most of us recognise that industrialised humanity has (largely unwittingly) brought on widespread and toxic destruction: of communities, of health and wellbeing, of myriad creatures who run, fly or swim, and crucially, the whole living planet that carries us all through space. 'Biophiles', those who love Life in all its forms, are responding to the accelerating destruction in diverse ways. There are plenty of resilient warriors fighting for environmental justice who thrive on battle, and are energised by duels of words and wits. Others can't wait to get out there and challenge the dominant paradigm, but don't have enough practical information. I didn't write this book for them: there are already numerous how-to books, and online resources such as *seedsforchange.org.uk*. Others engage in creative, pragmatic responses to today's chaos and destruction: they get on with the physical work of building, growing and developing the healthy society they want to see. They're busy creating initiatives which grow up like bright shoots through the crumbling global infrastructure of a post-capitalist economy – and many are thriving. They are farmers and craftspeople, builders and therapists, funeral directors and bakers. I salute these innovative, practical, energetic people; I send them much gratitude. But I didn't write this book for them, either: there are already plenty of online resources and how-to books about ethical living, such as Rob Hopkins' *The Power of Just Doing*. And there are plenty of gentle, concerned souls who have no wish to be warriors. Maybe they have plenty to worry about closer to home. Maybe they don't like the direction society is taking, but accept 'that's just how things are'. Some choose to simply embody and promote a life-enhancing, rather than life-destroying, economy in their private lives. All have a niche in our human ecosystem.

The Trembling Warrior celebrates and encourages all who feel drawn to speak truth to power, despite their reticence. It is for and about reluctant activists: those leaning over the edge of comfort, and those holding back; those who strive to walk a wise path between fear and action: the gentle visionaries and dreamers drawn more to humanity's place in the universe than practical tasks. Some help shape the future by challenging the delusional recent past; they actively challenge destructive behaviour, although they may tremble at the thought of it; others yearn to do so, but haven't yet found their voice. When there are so many courageous campaigners willing to march, stand on the front line, and risk arrest, tender souls may quietly plead: can't we stay away from battlefields? Here are five responses to that poignant plea:

- 'Heroes' can be sensitive and afraid too, but they are gifted with (or have developed) sufficient courage to say and do what they feel they must.

- Many gentle souls do indeed choose to stay behind the frontline doing whatever they do best, as we'll see. No-one can force you to step up, and you don't have to.

- Sometimes you may simply feel compelled to fight for what's right, even though you shrink from it; even though you may suffer in some way as a result.

- If you feel called to act courageously by something bigger than you, then it quite possibly needs you and your unique gift: perhaps for the very sensitivity you bring.

- You might love it!

Trembling, of course, isn't groundless. There are risks in challenging power based in selfishness, greed and corruption. We may also feel deeply uncomfortable challenging those unaware of the implications of their daily behaviours, their worldview having been shaped by mass marketing and corrupt media – whether directly, or inherited. Yet the time for respectful tolerance is over: self-destructive behaviours can't be ignored any more. Most of us feel a flutter of fear when we speak our truth: whether at Westminster or in the office; at the shopping centre or in the homes of friends and family. And sometimes the most uncomfortable one to confront is ourselves. But we can do all this, and more, if we are well-resourced.

Within these pages you'll find a smörgåsbord of stories from Trembling Warriors. They offer experience, inspiration, caution, and guidance; bringing comfort, affirmation and idea-sparking at a time when those standing up to defend vulnerable creatures and places are sent to prison as a warning to others. You'll find honest and heartfelt sharings from those who yearn to make a difference, but sometimes have trouble showing up - maybe because of the very sensitivity that tells them there's something seriously wrong with the direction humanity is taking. You'll meet ordinary people who've managed to create and put on their own personal armour, to stand up in all their vulnerability, and do what needs to be done.

In the first section we'll look at who Trembling Warriors are: the gifts they bring to the world, what motivates them, some characteristics they share, the struggles they encounter, and why they matter so much today. I don't claim the Trembling Warrior as a distinct personality type, or that it maps exactly on to any existing personality models (though readers familiar with C.J. Jung's work on personality, and those who have built on it, may recognise some themes). However, thinking about innate differences in ways of being human can help us understand why some people access certain traits so readily, while others naturally focus elsewhere. Doing so can ease a lot of unnecessary tension.

The second section explores more deeply some common qualities of the 'sensitive idealist'. These explorations are not intended as a comprehensive and accurate description of a blueprint personality: rather as an exploration of human themes intended to illuminate what sensitive idealists bring to the world - and why they sometimes struggle to bring it. The qualities explored all have their light and shadow: that is, they can manifest joyful and wonderful things in the world, but can also – especially borne out of awareness – cause trouble for Trembling Warriors and those around them. The purpose of this section is to offer readers an opportunity to recognise, own and begin to integrate those qualities or aspects that resonate most with them.

In the third section we'll explore diverse forms of activism. Some, you would expect to find; others may not have occurred to you as activism. You'll find discussion about the particular rewards and challenges of each, and personal stories of achievement, learning and disappointment. This section offers food for reflection if you're feeling the call, or the nudge, of that which you care passionately about. If you're hovering on the edge of doing something, trying to decide what sort of activism you'd enjoy most and be best at, these chapters may bring some clarity and resolve.

The fourth section is about resourcing yourself to sustain activism: to keep coming back and back and back, at a time when you are much needed. Sensitive activists tell how they look after themselves whilst being effective in the world, and there's wisdom and insight from therapists and healers who understand sensitive idealists: their qualities, their motivations, and the 'wounds' they're prone to. I hope this last part will help you gain a greater understanding of your own vulnerability, and how to transform it into something more resilient, beautiful, and empowered.

A quick word on idealism, which should not be confused with ideology: *ideology* is a 'science of ideas' – any ideas – on which people base their actions. *Idealism* is a vision of things as they could be: a version of perfection which will never come about, but is worth aspiring to anyway. The idealists I have in mind envisage a future in which all beings live in harmonious balance on a thriving planet. They are sometimes hopeful, sometimes desperate; sometimes visionary, sometimes naïve. But their contribution to community – whether local or global, human or otherwise – is essential. I explained in *Hearing our Calling* why I believe idealists are born for a reason: holding, as they do, the ethical end of a spectrum of possible futures – whose opposite pole is thoughtless destruction of life on Earth for short term gain.

Self-publishing has enabled me to write specifically for gentle idealists, and that in turn has liberated me to explore vulnerability far more openly than I might have if I was self-censoring, imagining the responses of readers who might shout 'snowflake', or attempting to reach and please everyone – which is of course impossible anyway. In the same spirit, those who've offered their stories have been generous and open-hearted. I hope the reading will be as nourishing, stretching, and enjoyable for you as the research and writing has been for me.

All authors necessarily write from the fertile ground of their own story. I had three powerful drivers in writing this book: an external motivation to encourage reluctant activists everywhere, an internal motivation to understand and more effectively express my own inner Trembling Warrior, and my ever-present, slow-burning desire and commitment to serve the world and its inhabitants in the best way I can. Some aspects of Trembling Warriorship described here are deeply familiar to me personally, and others less so; all have evolved, over the course of my life.

If you are on the path this book explores, you too may have grown up with the natural world as your solace, your playground and your paradise, and feel yourself to be deeply embedded in the biosphere. Perhaps you didn't get to play with other children when you were small, and formed strong familial bonds with animal and plant life: perhaps the only community you knew, where interaction and engagement were learned through following, touching, watching, and listening; living intimately with the birds in the hedges, and the tiny creatures moving between blades of grass. Or perhaps you had good reason in childhood for finding humanity too difficult to bear. You may have sought refuge in nature, where you wouldn't be punished, judged, humiliated or abused. Still others will have grown up in families where honouring and loving nature was just what you did. Before you even started school, you learned valuable lessons about the wild world, and your place within it. Or maybe you grew up in an urban environment, and a connection to nature has come as a later, unexpected, most welcome blessing. Maybe it hasn't come yet, but somewhere your soul yearns for it…

Although my own philosophy is deeply rooted in a love of the natural world, you may well identify with Trembling Warriorship through your love of humanity. It's all part of the same service: we are all nature.

Today, humans have the ability and technology (and, you might think, the desire) to wipe out not only itself, but most other species that sail on this beautiful blue planet. The stakes have never been higher. But our task is not to beat or obliterate mainstream society (even if such a thing were possible): rather to help co-create a future in which *all* creatures live well; where love for the natural world, currently considered 'alternative', is simply natural. That, as far as I can see, is the best hope for all of us.

A Trembling Warrior's Dream

I am standing on a high plateau, looking out over a broad landscape of forests, rivers, highways, winding paths, ceremonial sites, villages, cities, and mountains; with a glimpse of the Ocean beyond.

I perceive the landscape in its parts, but also as an integrated whole: I can intuit where the animal tracks lead, and why. I notice the colours of the fields changing, and somehow I know such a change heralds the melting of mountain snow. I see flames rising from a crack running through the moorland sweep of dry bracken, and I sense which way the wind is blowing. I see birds fleeing, fast, low and silent, toward the waters in the North, and I nod in understanding.

I'm watching people on the highways and in the cities as if from above: I can see their yellow smoke rising, and spreading across the sky. As I watch, it slowly coalesces beyond the mountain peaks into a dark storm that gains in strength as it begins to move slowly back towards the people. But I am too far away to warn them. I shout, but my voice is carried away on the wind. The few who do catch my words shake their heads: my urgent scream of 'Stop it!' means nothing to them. They return to sucking ancient oil from the body of the Earth: playing with it for a while, and then smearing it over her surface, flushing it into her oceans and burning it into the air that is the life breath of every living being.

And then I look down at my hands, and am bewildered and ashamed to find viscous black tar dripping from my fingers. I try to get it off, but I can't... I look up, and I see that the sky is turning gold. I am filled with a sense of peace.

Anon.

PART ONE

The Trembling Warriors

Trembling Warriors are those who feel called to stand up for all that is good in the world, although they feel vulnerable in doing so. They are the world's poets, artists and dreamers; healers, sages, and visionaries - even if they have not yet found a way to bring these gifts forward into their community. At the core of each Trembling Warrior is a deep and self-renewing conviction that a better world is possible. (The *world* is of course already very good, in endless rich, beautiful and astonishing ways. When we speak of changing the world, we invariably mean the human aspect!) Idealistic and gentle, Trembling Warriors feel compelled to address injustice and suffering: although they feel uncomfortable doing so, or trying to - or even considering it. The tenderness that vibrates to the cries of the Earth is raw and vulnerable to the aggression and exposure of today's society.

Trembling can arise from many sources. It's adrenaline surging through your body when you care enough about something to be angry, outraged, or defiant. It's the excitement of going into battle; it's the shock of conflict, or locked-away trauma; it's fear of climate change, or fishless oceans; fear of retribution, or rejection; or fear of being truly seen or heard. It's the mysterious transpersonal force that animates you as you move in service of the greater good. It's the visceral shock of seeing brutalised pigs in a factory farm, meeting starving pensioners in Armenia, witnessing the destruction of ancient woodland. It's the pounding of your heart as your time to speak out approaches. It's a passionate love of Life itself, flaring up in your whole being, ready to meet whatever it faces.

We are warriors not because we love war, but because we love our glorious living world, and we refuse to look away and let it be torn up, despoiled, and extinguished by the blindness and craving of a lost and hungry humanity. The mainstream, shaped by neoliberalist conformity, rejects what is vibrant and colourful, trammelled into the norm that grey is the only possible colour for your (compulsory) new soft furnishings, black the only colour for important events. Society swallows the lie that to have a hobby, to be joyfully enthusiastic about something, is *sad.* Yet under these brittle layers of cultural conditioning, what's truly sad is the loneliness of a world where targets, profit, and conformity count more than love, health, and joy. Trembling Warriors are prepared to name and defend these lost qualities: we reject the neoliberal narrative. We commit ourselves to challenging what we cannot accept, and often that means speaking truth to power. This we fear – and sometimes, rightly so... challenge can have serious consequences. Trembling Warriors may follow any of three paths:

- Feel moved by the pain of the world but hold back, and then feel troubled by the resulting inner conflict.

- Sublimate the angst, escaping the dire realities of the twenty-first century in *ungrounded* spirituality, and other escape activities.

- Actively engage with the Shadow in society and in ourselves, taking mature responsibility for the best creative response we can make, whenever we are able.

Trembling Warriors are all furious that the Earth's biosphere (every manifestation of life that exists around the globe) is being systematically exploited, controlled, pushed to the very edge of being. We feel profound sorrow about the knowledge of our complicity in the harm done. Yet Trembling Warriors are endlessly diverse; each of us is unique. So, some of the following words will resonate with you, and others will not quite stick...

You may have a great capacity for love and empathy, finding tremendous wonder and delight in the beauty of life, human or otherwise (for some, especially otherwise). You may enjoy an aptitude for creative expression: whether writing or story-telling, or making music, or art. You are compassionate: perhaps able to empathise with others, sometimes sensing what they're feeling or needing even before they know it themselves. Maybe you hold a strong vision of a better society, with an ever-renewing faith that the future you dream of can be brought into being. You may experience an inner sense of purpose – of vocation, even – about making your contribution to the greater good: whether through your work, spontaneous activities, or the way you live your life. Maybe you see unfolding global stories as if from afar: maybe you perceive and speculate about their complexity, and their possible futures. You have a strong sense of right and wrong; maybe you even call them 'good and evil'. You know in your heart, or in your bones, or in your soul, that humanity has gone astray and Life is being harmed. That same tenderness makes you personally vulnerable: whether to criticism, exclusion, conflict, humiliation, or rejection. So fighting for what you love can be difficult – especially today, when speaking out in public invites spiteful attacks, and long-held notions of right and wrong are not only out of fashion, but seem to be vanishing from society. Nevertheless, you feel compelled to speak out.

It can take courage to challenge the status quo: whether calling out fossil fuel companies, or simply daring to talk about climate change or plastic pollution in a neighbourhood, peer group or workplace that operates mostly under the spell of the mainstream. But the tide is turning: biophilia (love of Life) is at last beginning to be seen as normal again. It is bizarre, though not inexplicable, that doing so was ever considered 'alternative'. Thanks in part to David Attenborough, but also to countless passionate groups and individuals, many of them young, killing the planet is no longer socially acceptable.

We aren't all blessed with Sir David Attenborough's reach and influence. Gentle souls who put people before profit, and environment before economy, feel they lack the courage to take on their families or colleagues, never mind Life-trashing governments and corporations. Some of those most passionate about advocating for the non-human world seem least equipped to do so. As economies and climates unravel, Trembling Warriors experience an urgent need to *do something*. They may dream of going into battle, but tremble at the thought of confrontation. Yet they are richly equipped. Often, they simply need a little encouragement or support to play their part in the world's unfolding drama.

Whatever aspect of Life they care about, Trembling Warriors are prone to certain vulnerabilities. Some are too readily disempowered. Some feel disregarded and belittled by others – or even by themselves. Such shrinkage or implosion derives from inner fragility, gentleness or modesty; self-doubt, or vulnerable self-esteem. These traits are often rooted in our innate personality, and compounded by our childhood experiences.

Furthermore, some may feel diminished by social background, or how they present themselves to their community: how they dress, or how they speak: such markers are often used to make assumptions and judgments about whether a person is worth listening to or not. Some grew up learning that women can't have an opinion, let alone a strong one. Some grew up learning that men can't feel tender or afraid. Others may carry from a disfiguring, debilitating or disadvantaging condition, for example disability, depression or dyslexia: causing them to be seen as, or even believe themselves to be, 'less than' others (although in less conventional ways they are often much more). Some are of marginalised race or sexuality; in some countries, would-be warriors are legally barred from speaking out. Some work or live within a hierarchy where to protest from a lower rank is dangerous, or even impossible. But these silent voices contain a warrior's burning flame.

A Special Role

The role Trembling Warriors occupy, on the edge of society, is a special one. Overly humble Trembling Warriors may think that sounds grandiose. But although you didn't choose it, and may not even want it, you do occupy a special role of responsibility - *as does everyone else.* Evidently engineers, builders, and growers all make vital contributions to the world. The role of the Trembling Warrior is the most important, in that it intercedes with humans on behalf of the other-than-human: with soul, with creatures, nature spirits, or the land itself. *Yet an engineer also knows his or her work is the most important*: their skill provides infrastructure without which, in some regions, many would die. Indeed, engineers may naturally dismiss sensitive idealists as 'fluffy' (especially as they are seldom highly practical). They may not see much point in what we do; indeed, some can't even see what we do. And to the cook, his or her role is obviously what matters most: performing a brand of alchemy with raw ingredients to nourish bodies and delight senses. The same with the nurse... and so on. In a healthy society all contributions are precious, welcome, and necessary, and we can all stretch into other roles when there's a need. Idealists typically recognise and appreciate the contributions of others; doing so goes with the archetype. But others don't necessarily always see what Trembling Warriors bring, invisible as it often is. It is a role out of fashion with the mainstream. That's why we frequently need to remind ourselves, and each other, of the value and validity of our contribution.

Certain wild animals, and even the domestic cow, employ individuals to stand guard and raise the alarm if danger approaches. They necessarily occupy a space apart from their fellows: on the edge, scanning outward for threats, but still able to see the herd. Trembling Warriors also occupy a liminal space, but in a psychological or spiritual way rather than physically (though sometimes that too). The human being evidently has a different consciousness from other animals: not better, but different. Our technology has advanced so far that we hold a frightening amount of power: its exponential growth needs some human outriders (or outsiders) to keep an eye on our direction of travel. However, although we look outward, holding the wellbeing of all life in our intention – we find we must look inward, to our own 'herd', for the main source of danger: danger to the outer realm of life, and to the herd itself. The problem is that unlike the watch-cow, liminal humans struggle to be heard: in our peripheral position we're easily ignored, dismissed or excluded – or seen to be 'crying wolf'. (Of course, nobody likes a suggestion that they might actually *be* the wolf.)

A Long Tradition

Humanity has always produced advocates for non-human life, acting as a bridge between the two, inhabiting the margins of society. They have existed for thousands of years: often in the role of priest, wise elder, or healer: on the margins of the tribe but a central part of it nevertheless, granted visions which were trusted and honoured by others whose roles involved meeting practical needs. Communities needed the visionary as a sort of moral compass, to ensure they didn't corrupt the natural balance. Throughout civilisation there have been people outraged on behalf of other beings, striving to hold a line against the progress of unmitigated practicality towards destruction. It's likely that when the first fences were made to keep animals in one place for human use, someone gave impassioned oratories about where such a practice might lead. But sooner or later, they were ignored. Animals were enclosed, and declared *possessions* – and some people witnessing such an innovative exertion of control thought, what a good idea. This event, mundane though it may have seemed at the time, represents one of several pivotal moments: the rejection of wisdom that could have averted the immense suffering inflicted on animals and the planet by industrial farming, and the abandonment of a fragile, precious relationship of mutual respect, leading to the infinite varieties of abuse and destruction we see today, thousands of years after free animals became 'live stock'.

We can fairly safely imagine that there were reluctant activists protesting when vast stretches of medieval wild forest, and all the creatures who'd inhabited it over countless generations, fell victim to human need and greed. Those long-ago people may have sensed the impact: on individual living beings, and also the rich network of life. Perhaps their hearts cracked open as they saw what we had done. They might have tried to express their horror in language that might persuade arable farmers, or ship builders, focused as they were on meeting real and pressing requirements. Tree protector activists probably petitioned (without success) the rulers who demanded that the forest be cleared for food and fighting - as Trembling Warriors today attempt to protect the few trees they have left, in towns and cities where nature is seen by human-centric Councils not even as the enemy, but as inconvenient and superfluous.

In the early 1800s, Wiltshire-born author Richard Jefferies stepped out of the heady milieu of London journalism, and wrote with enraptured detail about the abundant creatures who played, fed, mated, and died alongside humans at home and work in and around his childhood village (now engulfed by Swindon). He recorded, with a fearful eye to the future, the brutal impact of a 'steam ploughing engine' on a countryside whose loudest sounds until then had been thunderstorms, and the racket of geese.

> 'Jerking forward, tearing its way through stubble and clay... it gives an idea of power which cannot but impress the mind. The broad wheels sink into the Earth under the pressure; the steam hissing from the escape valves is carried by the breeze through the hawthorn hedge, hiding the red berries with a strange, unwonted cloud; the thick dark brown smoke, rising from the funnel as the stoker casts its food of coal into the fiery mouth of the beast, falls again and floats heavily over the yellow

> stubble, smothering and driving away the partridges and hares. There is a smell of oil, and cotton-waste, and gas, and steam, and smoke, which overcomes the fresh, sweet odour of the earth and green things after a shower.

Jefferies died aged thirty-eight in relative poverty, having completed what was possibly the first post-apocalyptic novel, *After London*, in which a minutely described rewilding of England has taken place: 'And those whose business is theology have pointed out that the wickedness of those times surpassed understanding, and that a change and sweeping away of the human evil that had accumulated was necessary, and was effected by supernatural means.' Jefferies refused literary patronage as an insult to his creativity. As is true with plenty more visionaries, posthumous sales of his writing could have paid for a comfortable life several times over. Trembling Warriors don't walk an easy path.

The Wounded Healer

Today, Trembling Warriors have their work cut out as never before. They seek to defend health and happiness not only for themselves but for all beings, in the teeth of dangerous politicians, and powerful entities whose profit-seeking activities damage physical and mental health, threaten biodiversity and inflict multiple sicknesses on the planetary ecosystem. However, we are many, and our diverse passions meet and address such threats at all levels. We each care and advocate for what we love most: whether for humanity, or for birds, oceans, tigers, or wilderness. And for some, often but not always the older ones, it's all these and more.

'Liminal guardian' roles may no longer be recognised or valued by the mainstream, but plenty are called to it nevertheless. And they can have a hard time in the 21st century, whether they answer the call or not. As we've moved further away in time from the wisdom and skill of those on the edge of the village, such characters continue to be born into society, but those carrying the archetype usually receive little or no guidance in their youth (though as we will see later, that's starting to change). They've had to do their best: sometimes uninformed, sometimes naïve, sometimes lacking a convincing voice... but trying anyway. And sometimes in despair they declare themselves mad, or flawed, and give up. Trembling Warriors don't choose their path. In fact, it usually feels as though the path has chosen them. In *Hearing Our Calling*, I explained why I believe personal vocation to be innate: within a tribe (any group of humans), nature strives to provide a balance appropriate to the community's environmental and social context by providing the right mix of qualities and aptitudes. Our bodies cohere in the same way: every organ, every type of cell, every hormone, each with its role, contributing when needed to in a dynamic, self-regulating whole; every part called to make its unique contribution by fluctuations and arising conditions in the greater context. Ecosystems operate like this too, with each living being contributing their function (their gift) to a complex web of inter-relationship always striving for harmonious balance. The same process happens even with the planet as a whole living system. Gaia's constituent parts: rainforest, ocean currents, plate tectonics, weather patterns and the biotic community, are all connected and dependent on one another. At every level, all have an essential role to play. It's largely because we've lost sight of this basic principle that our species has got itself into trouble.

In the myth of Chiron, the centaur had an incurable wound inflicted by a poisoned arrow. Chiron gives us the archetypal role of the 'Wounded Healer': someone who suffered significant emotional pain in childhood, which led them to the healer's work, partly in an attempt to heal themselves. The wound is often exactly what makes it possible for the therapist to provide a transformative container for another's pain. The wounded healer archetype, although usually recognised in relation to therapists, is often found in those who seek to heal the natural world. But if we are to do this work well, our own healing needs to be taking place at the core of our endeavours.

In the same way that any eco-system is comprised of a fluctuating tapestry of different species, all contributing something unique and essential to the greater whole, humanity is made up of different types of personality, all with something vital to contribute. In the next part we'll take a look at some 'sensitive idealist' qualities that Trembling Warriors bring to the world; qualities that naturally equip us for inhabiting the world. Like all qualities, they have their flipsides, and we'll look at those too. We'll discover how others with differing personalities might experience us, and explore how our strengths can manifest in ways we'd rather they didn't. Sensitive idealists are all the same, all different, and all unique: some aspects will naturally resonate with you more than others.

Trembling Warriors may relate to most or all of the traits explored here. But all human beings can potentially access their 'inner Trembling Warrior'. For example, an activist may be naturally detached, logical and analytical in their action on behalf of Life. But with well-developed access to their emotions, they are just as able to bawl with grief, fear the spotlight, or show great care.

My aim is not to ascribe labels: I hope to encourage all readers to develop their 'sensitive idealist' qualities. Such qualities are largely absent, rejected or repressed today, and the grave consequences of that are playing out in the human story. I also invite reluctant activists to develop their less preferred aspects; to flex the muscles that can seem to belong exclusively to other sorts of people. We as a species have grown psychologically sophisticated and capable enough to develop all aspects of ourselves. We could blossom into a rounded, truly mature humanity, able to play the reciprocal, mutually enhancing role within the web of Life we did in pre-rational times, but with an extra dimension of consciousness. We are equipped with all we need to bring it about, but industrialised humans have lost sight of soul wisdom, and of the bigger picture we inhabit. That is why the Sensitive Idealist in all of us is called to pull humanity out of its current trajectory through soul wisdom and love.

A Trembling Warrior's Poem

There is a pain
floating fluently beneath
this cursed concrete
boiling geysers erupt
in place of fountains
wood pigeons used to cool
their fumbling feathers in.
I see them everywhere
scorched tatters
in the searing, hardened air
that presses against
my throbbing eardrums.
I see them scattered
on arid ground
desiccated souls drinking
the only fluid to be found.
As we gather
heat rises
from bleeding wounds
fumes blind our eyes
covered and bone-dry
until thunder stumbles upon us
clandestine Dust sparkles
particles scintillate
fire in the long awaited rain
polarities clash to wash away
our inured masks like clay
crumble in the redeeming flood.

At last
we quiet and stay

open

simple

fragile in trust

Klara Papp

Dreamer

At the core of Trembling Warriors is a deep and self-renewing conviction that a better world is possible. Idealists dream, even though we know may only be a dream, of paradise.

Optimism is coded into Trembling Warriors – although those around us may not always experience us that way. Assailed every day by endless causes for despair, we don't hold back from crying out to our people that our ship is about to sail off the edge of the world. Yet still we return to an underlying faith in a plot twist, and a happy ending. In various narratives, human consciousness will evolve to the next level, ushering in the real 'new age' of peace for all beings; or all the bad guys will be wiped out, leaving a small group of post-apocalyptic sad-but-wiser humans to begin anew; or humanity (Gaia's cancer) will be eradicated, leaving the planet to the creatures who manage to survive our ultimate self-destructive onslaught, as the planet rebalances herself in a new phase of evolution. Despite multiple systemic crises, our dream of a better future is unquenchable.

Trembling Warriors also tend to take an idealistic approach to the project of Self. Nurturing a belief in a better version of themselves, they undertake endless personal growth activities: workshops on which to discover their true calling, reading to grow wise, meditation or prayer to elevate their souls. They attend to the shortcomings of humanity on behalf of the species, but are also usually aware of their own imperfections, and strive constantly for enlightenment, or at least individuation.

Aspiring to the ideal, Trembling Warriors can hold back from speaking in case what they say isn't perfect, worrying that others will see their imperfection. We certainly wish to express ourselves as skilfully and authentically as we can, in service of our work. All over social media there are beautiful, encouraging memes created by and for tender idealists. Such words and images exhort us to believe in ourselves: to trust that what we are is sufficient. But you can't just flick a switch – if only it were so easy. Even a capacity for self-belief can never be quite good enough, and is often a lifelong work-in-progress. Sometimes the best you can do is recognise and honour what beauty and skill there is in what you have created, acknowledge and accept its imperfection, and know when to put your work out there anyway.

I had a friend who wanted to work as a therapist, but his fear of not being good enough meant he could never trust himself to be sufficiently skilled. Nor could he ever find a teacher or mentor he considered good enough, so his undoubted knowledge and talent lay underused and underdeveloped, while he did environmentally destructive work he could perform easily, but didn't enjoy. Another friend wrote a book but spent twenty years refining and tweaking it, so that when it eventually came out, much of what she had wanted to say no longer felt new. There's something here about walking a line: not rushing the work and putting it out before it's ready, but equally knowing when it's good enough, and letting go of an attachment to the idea of 'perfect'. To avoid either error, it helps to be aware of which you're most prone to.

Idealism, although it can hold you back, is of service to the world: especially in the Trembling Warrior's work (which, for many, is indivisible from the rest of life). Looking for and anticipating the best in people, we are often catalysts for others, who respond to a vision of their best selves like plants opening to warm sunshine. However, not everyone can respond to our dream for them – and not everyone wants to. Inevitably, dreamers are regularly disappointed. We're frequently forced to confront and acknowledge the less desirable aspects, or the shadow, of a person or organisation we'd been idealising (sometimes including ourselves). Idealists have to face it when others fail to hear and respond to our exhortations to action which will (we hope) make the world happier and healthier. We can't understand why everyone doesn't want a better world... until we realise others' version of a better world looks very different than ours. It can slip off our radar that many are simply struggling to get by in the world which *does* exist, and don't have the time or energy to even start thinking beyond the next day about what it *could* be like.

When idealists go public on an issue they care about passionately, chances are they'll be charged with hypocrisy at some point. We've all been asked questions such as, "How can you say you're a vegetarian when you're wearing leather boots?" Most people would like to believe perfect characters do exist. Notions of moral perfection sometimes reside in the unconscious shadow of those who don't have an idealist temperament. Projected on to idealists, such a quality might be despised, secretly coveted, or regarded with curious fascination (just as idealists might treat the projected quality of authority). Not infrequently, Trembling Warriors accuse each other of hypocrisy. We can feel let down when someone we assumed shares – and perhaps exceeds – our own ethical standards turns out not to be perfect after all. Hoping others embody the ideals we yearn towards, dreamers are serially disappointed. Yet we continue to dream. In the sobering but grounding the words of Aldo Leopold:

> "We shall never achieve harmony with the land, any more than we shall achieve absolute justice or liberty for people. In these higher aspirations the important thing is not to achieve but to strive."

In both their outer and inner lives, Trembling Warriors are prophets and ushers of twin futures: Transcendence and Doom. If you don't resource yourself well, anxiety that 'Nothing I can do is enough' could paralyse you from taking action at all – or it could force you to keep doing and doing and doing until you collapse in a heap, weary and bitter. However, the idealist's optimism is a key aspect of their role in society; an element of the task they were born for. If no-one was striving for a version of Utopia, any future resembling such a thing would certainly never come about. As long as there are idealists dreaming ardently towards good outcomes for the biosphere, those outcomes remain in potential, like seeds. Your dreams, even though they aren't always recognised as such, are your priceless gift to humanity.

The high ideals Trembling Warriors aspire to are not only unachievable, but unknowable. When you hold to these ideals uncompromisingly, nobody and nothing can ever be quite enough for you; indeed, you can never be quite enough for yourself. For dreamers, an uncomfortable but healing aspect of maturing is becoming able to truly accept your own and others' imperfections. If idealists were to accept and embrace their imperfections, might others acknowledge and aspire to their ideals, the whole naturally and organically finding a more integrated balance?

Tender Plant

Sensitivity enervates many a Trembling Warrior, tenderising both their perceptive senses and their emotions. Like plants that close up self-protectively in certain conditions, they instinctively recoil from harsh noises, lighting or fabrics. They might wince at the sight, or the sound, of violence. In this respect, there is little distinction between 'real' and 'fictional': although we are logically quite aware of the difference, the impact is the same. Maybe you can only stand high-energy environments such as parties, networking events and concerts for so long. Maybe you avoid places like fairgrounds and shopping malls, knowing it takes effort not to be overwhelmed by, or lost in, sensory input: pulsing lights of so many colours and rhythms, songs and sounds blaring from all directions, the sweet and synthetic smells, all the faces, the dynamic flow of energetic interactions. Heightened sensitivity attempts to take it all in and make meaning of it, in just the same way that a sheepdog, on seeing sheep, cannot help but begin rounding them up. It's simply what we do.

Most Trembling Warriors could be described as biophiles: lovers of Life, attuned to wellbeing. They sense the health (or otherwise) of an elderly man sitting on the pavement, a café table-top plant, a cow crossing the road to the milking parlour, a wildflower meadow. Many are committed to improving the lot of humanity through projects such as foodbanks, preventing deportations, or championing minority groups. Others focus more on the other-than-human. Jerome Bernstein's *Living in the Borderland* is a landmark psychology textbook, in which he describes people (Borderlanders) who have a particular high attunement to non-human life. Such open awareness to the presence of other beings can bring great joy and delight; when all is well, our days are rich and blessed. But we feel harm acutely too, and in the last few centuries we haven't had to look very far to find harm. A Trembling Warrior's body vibrates to suffering: images of starving children, footage of orphaned orang-utans, or the sight and sound of a living hedgerow hacked by indiscriminate tractor-mounted machinery. You may even be acutely aware as you gouge the seeds out of a pepper...

I believe everyone has their inner Highly Sensitive Person, no matter how hidden; and everyone is potentially capable of biophilia. I believe it's possible that we all even have an inner Borderlander; indeed, Bernstein reports that he and his supervisees are seeing increasing numbers of nature-sensitive clients in their consulting rooms. For most people, though, nature-sensitivity is either naturally less preferred in favour of other affinities, or is actively suppressed. Trembling Warriors carry such awareness uppermost (if not always outermost).

These are particularly agonising times for both human-loving philanthropists and nature-loving Borderlanders to live through. They can feel overwhelmed by relentless atrocities and wonder, what's the point in even trying to make a difference? Yet even as they are battered by constant shock and disappointment, their optimism is ever-renewing that a gentle humanity could still be possible: that the whole species could even ascend to an unprecedented level of consciousness as we emerge from chaos. Trembling Warriors see brutality marching inexorably into every sacred place, and the fire of our love for the natural and beautiful flares up in indignant rage and resistance. We feel the pain, and we want it to stop. The urge to curl up our petals is strong, but we override it, forcing them to stay open. We ask, what can we do? Or, in a less hypothetical and more empowered way, we ask what we can do.

Trembling Warriors have it in our nature not only to sense states of wellbeing, but also to defend and enhance them. That's why we are drawn to be active in places (real or virtual) where people gather, when introverts especially would much rather be sitting by a stream, or reading poetry, or painting, or enjoying emotional intimacy. We may yearn for an imagined time when assaults on Life were rarer, or of far smaller scale; when humans lacked the technology to inflict the damage now so commonplace.

We know, of course, that predation, violence, cannibalism, torture, infanticide, starvation, parasitism and slavery are rife, and take place amongst non-human species too. But we'd much rather they didn't. Videos of animal co-operation, altruism, cross-species friendships, monogamous pairs, and tender child-raising are delightful and comforting. We share them as evidence not only of animal sentience, but of how humanity could be. We attempt to live so as not to inflict suffering on any other being, and our inevitable failure to do so can bring debilitating pain and guilt. Innate sensitivity renders us more vulnerable than most to criticism, rejection, exclusion, conflict and ridicule. We may have grown bark over some of these tender places, either soft or brittle or spiny – or maybe they were left raw and stinging.

Trembling Warriors tend to internalise hurts: partly in a hope to preserve good relations so we are not plunged into isolation, low self-esteem, shame, or despair, but also because it goes against our nature to inflict discomfort on the other. Holding back so as not to hurt or inconvenience people is often regarded as psychologically unhealthy, but is in fact a natural trait of the sensitive idealist, bringing widely welcomed and much-needed (and sometimes abused) compassion and empathy to society. Self-abnegation causes imbalance only when a desire to serve others' wellbeing eclipses awareness of your own needs. It's all about conscious choice.

Sensitivity isn't, of course, exclusive to artistic types. Gaby is a volunteer who naturally organises people. In the various projects she supports, she often tells others what they should be doing, and how they should be doing it. She's very good at what she does, but inevitably her 'helpful' approach raises hackles. When colleagues lash back she finds it hurtful, and can worry for days – although she only admits that to a very few, disliking what she sees as 'weakness'. She avoids the news, because she can't bear to witness suffering. Gaby *makes decisions* using detached logic, but nevertheless sensitivity plays a significant part in her lived experience. Everyone is *capable* of feeling deeply... but emotions guide sensitive idealists' lives. Their particular rawness means they are also more likely to be viscerally disturbed by adverse experiences such as conflict, or harsh feedback.

In the not-so-distant past, sensitive members of a community were sometimes affectionately called delicate or tender flowers, implying they were to be cherished and nurtured for their beauty and rarity, even if the care they needed to thrive could be irritating. Today, in a society taught ruthless competition, mistrust and individuality, sensitivity is projected on to a few. Naturally, carrying all that tenderness can be hard to bear. It must often stay hidden if we're to survive - and not only in a hardened workplace. Eighty-six-year-old Jane remembers:

> "I worked for about thirteen years as a church volunteer, with the encouragement & support of the clergy: even so, my self-confidence was drained by the total rejection of my presence among the congregation - 'Northerners are not acceptable to Home Counties ladies' - but I carried on with some innovative work. Then we had a change of clergy. There was no support for lay volunteers, and I was still frozen out of the coffee mornings. My ability to contribute to work with the teenagers just faded."

In the more stringent parts of the 'system', putting compassion before efficiency is considered dereliction of duty. And if you melt down, you probably deserve it for being 'too sensitive'. But sensitivity is not redundant yet. As long as humanity cannot imagine itself without altruism, mercy, and kindness, there is a place for tender flowers.

Hedge-dweller

If you've spent any time outside sitting quietly and just watching, you'll have noticed that some creatures boldly use open spaces, while others, such as mice, wrens, and dunnocks, stay within the protection of the hedgerow, emerging from the undergrowth only when they have to.

Hedge-dwellers are keeping themselves safe from predators, and reluctant activists sometimes need to do this too. Of course, the predators they fear are usually other humans. To protect yourself you might hide on the edge of social media, in corners of rooms, or behind the stage. You may simply refrain from speaking – although you have thoughts arising, asking to be spoken.

We know other humans aren't (usually) likely to kill us. Timidity is often rooted more in issues of status and self-worth: both of which could spell life or death for our ancestors. However, Trembling Warriors' self-doubt can spring from concerns not only about personal status and safety, but also whether they will even be heard. Self-doubt can also come from a wish to be more wise and eloquent than is always possible, and from a lack of certainty that what we want to say is accurate or acceptable.

Self-doubt hopes to protect us from the uncomfortable or even debilitating guilt, embarrassment or shame of 'getting it wrong'. These three emotions are powerful forms of self-recognition, tools of conscience which keep us all in line with our community – but Trembling Warriors are particularly susceptible to them. Shame, the most powerful of the three, is usually hidden, and for good reason: it makes us vulnerable. And when we feel vulnerable, we want to hide.

Hiding, as David Whyte says in his beautiful book *Consolations,* is underestimated. It is a way of staying alive; of holding ourselves until we are ready to come into the light.

> 'We live in a time of the dissected soul, the immediate disclosure; our thoughts, imaginings and longings exposed to the light too much, too early and too often,

> our best qualities squeezed too soon into a world already awash with ideas which oppress our sense of self and our sense of others. What is real is almost always to begin with, hidden, and does not want to be understood by the part of our mind which mistakenly thinks it knows what is happening. What is precious inside us does not care to be known by the mind in ways that diminish its presence.
>
> Hiding is an act of freedom from the misunderstanding of others, especially in the enclosing world of oppressive secret government and private entities, attempting to name us, to anticipate us, to leave us with no place to hide and grow in ways unmanaged by a creeping necessity for absolute naming, absolute tracking and absolute control. Hiding is a bid for independence, from others, from mistaken ideas we have about our selves, from an oppressive and mistaken wish to keep us completely safe, completely ministered to, and therefore completely managed. Hiding is creative, necessary and beautifully subversive of outside interference and control.'

There are times for hiding, and times for emerging. Hedge-dwellers can be enticed out of hiding: to feed, to find other hedge-dwellers, or simply to enjoy some sunshine on their bodies. Trembling Warriors do well to know when it's time to hide, but also when it's time to emerge. In these days of upheaval, we're called to emerge more often, or for longer, than the introverts among us might like. But industrialised humanity has drifted so far from natural care and responsibility for people and planet, there's now more shame in calling someone out for their carbon-emitting lifestyle than there is shame for contributing to irreversible climate change. Extraversion (turning our energy outwards) helps to express our dreams for a better future. Remember, even if extraversion isn't your most natural way of being, you do have access to it. It can be grown and strengthened through both soul work, and actual practise.

The God Pan lived – or lives – in the wild forest. It is said that whenever a villager leaves home on their own, as they reach the edge of the forest Pan lays a hairy hand on their shoulder, whispering, "Are you sure you want to do this? Who are you, to be leaving the village? Are you sure you are on the right path? How do you know you will survive?" Such questions naturally raise self-doubt, and at this point many turn and run back to the comfort of the village, as a mouse bolts to a small, dark place with a thumping heart.

Pan offers a choice: "Give up your dream of stepping out into the world with your unique voice and your dreams, and you will still have a place in the village. You won't necessarily be happy, but you will be safe; at least, for now. Or stride further into the wild woods, and learn to encounter the mysteries you will surely meet. You will find you are not alone, after all. Only this way can you offer yourself fully to the unfolding story of the world."

Hedge-dwellers are not hedge-bound. At certain times a dunnock will stand on the top branches, singing its high and earnest message in all directions. And when all that's precious to the wren is threatened, it often deliberately makes itself vulnerable in plain sight, in a courageous bid to protect what it loves. In section four, we'll explore how Trembling Warriors can resource themselves to carry their message to their fellow humans, and protect what they love. But whenever your heart thumps unbearably, remember (as if you could forget) that the quiet, hidden places beneath the hedgerow await you...

Frightened Doe

Most Trembling Warriors are by definition familiar with fear (an emotion that's a step up from the self-doubt of the hedge-dweller). Fear is what motivates many reluctant activists, at a time when there is so much to be fearful about. Some fight passionately against climate change not out of tenderness, or a vision of Utopia, but from a primal, very natural fear of their own death. And some are fearful of activism itself.

In the late eighties, I had a friend who'd been suffering from agoraphobic panic attacks. At that time *Feel the Fear and Do It Anyway* by Susan Jeffers was a bestseller. My friend read it, and was hugely inspired to make positive changes in her life. I was happy for her, but uneasy about the title. Fear has a really, really important role. If self-doubt wants to keep us safe, fear wants to keep us alive. Any of what are usually called 'negative emotions' exist to let us know that we're out of balance, and some creative adjustment is needed.

Many Trembling Warriors are only too familiar with their inner 'frightened doe'. Sometimes the fear is unwarranted, springing from a bodily expectation of repercussions we learnt to anticipate when we were small. Totally dependent on the adults in our lives, we knew a primal terror of 'getting it wrong' – particularly if we felt ourselves loved only conditionally. If we were to be abandoned as a result of offending parental authority, we would die – or we would not be loved, which was just as terrifying a prospect. As we grow into more self-reliant adults ourselves, we have less to dread: we are not so vulnerable. But memories of responses which kept us loved and safe can hold on, long past a time when they've ceased to be useful. We can look not only to our own past but also to human history for the roots of fear, in the 'fight or flight' response to apparent threat. When you stand up to speak to a crowd, you may consciously fear their judgment – but your ancient limbic system is remembering the rush and attack of a predatory enemy. As an adult in today's society, feeling fear and doing something anyway is a good strategy for anyone nervous about speaking to a crowd, challenging your MP, or refusing an unethical gift.

But of course, not all fears are unwarranted. To risk stating the obvious, risks have possible uncomfortable consequences. Let's say you've walked past the cleaning cupboard in your office, and seen the shelves stocked with cleaning fluids you wouldn't dream of pouring down your own drains and out into the waterways, because you understand the harm to aquatic life. Raising it with the facilities team could lead to a policy that's better for waterways; or it could result in defensiveness, dismissal and exclusion – which makes life particularly hard if you dislike conflict, or don't handle rejection well. You could be seen as whistleblowing; and in some companies, you might even risk losing your job if you push it too hard.

When you dare to offend authority – a risk in most types of activism – some trembling is quite natural. But it's quite another matter to force yourself into something your body's ancient wisdom is screaming 'no' to. When you shut out that inner voice, ignore the flashing alarm, you mistake your wilful deafness and blindness for courage – especially if another voice, usually a critical one, is nagging that you 'should' do this or the other thing. Sensitive idealists sometimes believe we *must* make ourselves vulnerable in order to make a difference. But that stern judgmental voice doesn't usually serve us, or the greater good. Furthermore, we can be rather too good at accommodating others: making their behaviour alright with ourselves when it really isn't, and calling it inclusivity. In such situations, the real courage is in finding the ability to say no when no it is; to set your own boundaries with clarity, and deploy them with confidence.

The wisdom (as usual) is in knowing the difference: is the trembling arising from your inner trembling doe who needs soothing and encouraging, or your intuitive alarm system that needs heeding? We'll explore later how a crucial aspect of soul work is developing ever more intimate familiarity with your own individual organism: your complex psyche, and your body that is a physical expression of your psyche. Our bodies give us very accurate indications, and learning to tune in to their message is well worth it.

Awareness of context is another precious ingredient for clarity about what's 'right' and what's 'wrong' for you. Here's one question to ask yourself when you have a physical resistance to stepping up: "Am I the one needed for this? Or is someone else already on it, or will step up if I step back?" In *Wild Mind,* Bill Plotkin suggests further questions, all valuable for reluctant activists: 'What is dangerous and therefore to be escaped, avoided, or approached cautiously? What do I need to do to protect myself or others? What degree of risk is tolerable in pursuit of which goals? Given that zero risk is deadening, what degree of risk is optimal?' There aren't always clear answers. We can never know what is going to happen, and we can never know what would have happened. The reluctant activist's dance with fear of exposure, restraint, or retribution is an ongoing experiment bringing rich experience which can inform our future actions - when we pay aware attention.

Sally couldn't decide whether to take the stage and share a story at an event: her experience might help others, but it felt deeply personal. As she spoke about her dilemma, Sally's hands went to her face, and then to her ribs. I invited her to check in with what her body was telling her, and she said almost straight away, "No, it's too exposing. I don't have to do it." As she spoke these words, her body relaxed with relief, and she began to talk about another project. The next time I saw Sally, she told me that encouraged by others, she'd changed her mind and done the talk after all. It had been a powerfully positive experience for her: not just the telling of her story, but the affirmation she experienced on receiving warm feedback from the audience. Giving herself permission *not* to speak had made it possible for her to decide she would.

Michelangelo is popularly reputed to have said, 'The danger is not that you aim high and miss, but that you aim low and hit.' These words are often used to encourage us to reach, stretch, achieve more, fulfil our potential. Fair enough. Every day, there are people who take a risk, aim high, and are delighted and amazed by what they manage to achieve. Aiming low and hitting can nurture complacency, stagnating personal growth. *But the danger of aiming high and missing is also very real.* Taking yourself out of your depth without the right preparation, support or personal resilience can bash your confidence, self-worth and sense of identity. It can lead to burnout, trauma, nervous breakdown, depression, or anxiety from which it can take years to recover - and these conditions can have ongoing physical symptoms too. Step out of your comfort zone by all means, but have a strategy for getting back to it if you find yourself in too deep. And remember, every time you step out of your comfort zone, it grows a little...

Fire

There is a fire at the heart of all Trembling Warriors; otherwise they would not be warriors at all. They would simply accede to despair or resignation. In some it burns clearly and brightly, but for natural introverts it is a well-concealed flame - one that can be all too easily extinguished by images of receding sea ice, or personal criticism, or a sense of having failed. You can see it when the light has gone out of a Trembling Warrior's eyes. Those around them feel it when their bold, if flickering, glow is absent. But the embers are hot, and can easily be restoked by love, fear or anger - or all three together. Sooner or later, the flame leaps back into life in response to a gust of exhortation, drawn out by an incendiary situation. The world says, "You are needed!" and the Trembling Warrior's fire rises in response.

The introvert Trembling Warrior's flame is their surprising gift to the world. They are usually warm but mild, often to the extent that others don't take them seriously. When we are attempting to be effective, we are experienced and perceived very differently if we let others see the intensity of our flame. It can be used to illuminate a dark corner or to ignite a lover; to warm a chilled soul, or light a blaze in another reluctant activist. Most of the time, gentle idealists wield the tools of peace, love, and wisdom. But when they need it most - or when the world needs it most - their fire is readily summoned: indeed, it often comes roaring up unbidden. Such heat and intensity can be extraordinary to see. I've witnessed it in a young man telling the story of Parsifal late one night with sparks in his eyes; in the spitting coals of a teacher who felt himself insulted; in the flaring ire of an old woman outraged by the dishonesty of the system. You feel it when the attention of a lit-up audience reaches out to meet your words, or when a poker is deliberately thrust into a part of you that's tender and exposed.

Such a powerful gift should be used wisely. Otherwise it can do great harm: to others, and to the wielder. Most Trembling

Warriors know this to their cost: as the burner, and as the burnt. Maria spent many youthful years fighting for social justice in Spain. In her dissertation about activism and burnout, she wrote regretfully about the conflict she ignited in her family.

> "I carried my activism with anger and violence within, in a rigid mind not capable of understanding others' positions, including a great part of my family. I became frustrated with the long process of change, and sceptical that we would ever achieve it… my whole self was a paradox in motion, calling for a caring, loving world while shouting at those who did not understand and follow."

If you're overly self-consciousness about your own vulnerability, you may imagine others don't feel pain (or any other passion) as acutely, or as often, as you do. You may not recognise your own power to hurt – especially if your elders hid their pain from you as you grew up. Until and unless we have learnt otherwise, we can be paradoxically prone to engulfing others with fire, in an unconsidered and erroneous belief that they are somehow invulnerable – and that we are more vulnerable than we actually are. We can over-defend. At its most destructive, the Trembling Warrior's fire is used with fierce intention to hurt others in retaliation for hurts our tender ego believes itself to have suffered, when no harm was intended (or at least, less harm than we imagined).

When we don't know how to steward our fire wisely, it is as prone to being killed as it is to killing. If we haven't learned to guard our flame well, we can neglectfully allow it to be blown out by cold gusts of criticism, rejection or self-doubt – exactly when we need it most, to shine its golden light into some dark corridor of power, or to defend against a genuine personal threat. What we possess is a real-life light sabre; a 21st century staff. It can only be truly effective when wielded not only with self-belief, but with a sure sense of being in flow; in service of Life.

Fire is often associated with youth. One seventy-four-year-old said her son had been a passionate activist since he was in his teens. Following an unconventional path, he'd had an 'interesting life' but had never established a conventional career, and wasn't a success in mainstream terms. But his activism, although unpaid, had helped to bring about significant changes. His mother said, "I had been wondering if he was ever going to grow out of this rebellious phase. But after one particular phone call I hung up and thought no, he's right; we should all be doing this."

My own fire is kindled when someone tells me I shouldn't be angry with a person who repeatedly harms their fellow humans, or other creatures, or the living biosphere (in effect, criticising me for criticising others). If I must be angry, they say, then be angry with the *system*; I should not direct my anger towards any one person. I understand they're encouraging me to practice compassion: to blame (if I must blame at all) neoliberalism, or the false distinction between humans and nature that leads to abuse. But whilst I am sick of both, they are too nebulous to be satisfactory recipients of my anger. We can all blame the *system*, whilst failing to take (and accord) personal responsibility.

I advocate non-violent protest, consensus-seeking conversation, and leading by example. Most people know me as peaceful. But of course, I am sometimes angry: in fact just this morning, with a man wheeling tightly crated decoy ducks to be tethered on a French beach, to enable the shooting of wild ducks attracted by the panicked squawks. Call it love, call it projection, call it what you like; but it makes me wild enough to shout, "Can't you see they're terrified?" His reaction is whatever it is. I can't tell; he glances at me, and looks away. He might dismiss me as hysterical, or fail to understand me, or ignore me completely. But... another's anger (as Trembling Warriors well know) can also lead to shame, and a revision of behaviour. That is how, as a society, we self-regulate. Like fear, anger exists for a reason. It has its place, as does shame. Suppressing anger can be unhealthy for mind and body – and society.

Aristotle is often quoted as saying ‘Anybody can become angry; that is easy. But to be angry with the right person, to the right degree, at the right time, for the right purpose, and in the right way - that is not within everybody's power, and is not easy.’ Wise use of the flame does not come naturally. When to damp it down, when to hide it, when to fan it, when to simply step back, and let it through to do its work? For Trembling Warriors this is ongoing learning; a life’s work-in-progress. But Aristotle also said, ‘Know thyself’, and it’s a good place to start.

Puer / Puella

There is often something childlike about gentle idealists. Delighting in a rich connection with nature and the cosmos, they can be found walking through life in a state of wonder and eagerness: gazing at rainbows, singing a simple harmony, and trailing their fingers in dewy grasses. The 'perpetual child' archetype, sometimes manifest in Trembling Warriors, is known as the 'Puer' or 'Puella'. Those around such individuals are often charmed by their embodiment of innocence and goodness. With these qualities increasingly scarce, society often projects its disavowed, inherent innocence and goodness on to the Puer-Puella figure, where they can be enjoyed (or criticised as naïve) from a safe distance. Carrying innocence and wonder on behalf of the world, keeping them alive in bitter, cynical times, is a role whose importance can't be overstated.

A Puer or Puella sees the best in people, and gives their trust readily. Mostly their openness is repaid in spades, but occasionally their trust is naïvely misplaced, and trouble ensues. The Puer or Puella may become more discerning as result, but never really loses their ability to trust. Some, though, may respond by attempting to avoid being part of society. It's understandable, in a culture that's hard for gentle souls to bear. And sometimes it's necessary, as we've seen, to occupy a role on the edge of society. But being *on the edge* isn't the same as being *outside* (which, as humans, we can never truly be). Psychologist Jerome Bernstein's 'Borderlanders', with their attunement to non-human life, are particularly prone to seeing themselves as separate from society, even despising the human race. To despise those who harm what we love is also understandable. But such a childlike generalisation misses the whole glorious, chaotic mix that is our species: full as it is of shadow and light, meanness and generosity, cruelty and compassion. The joy of humanity can be a delightful, unfolding surprise (and relief) for idealists who thought they hated people. Larch Maxey has been a dedicated activist for most of his life. One of his earliest memories (one that can still move him to tears) is of taking toy farm animals from their indoor environment and setting them down in the soft green moss growing on the roof outside his window. He's been committed to service of wellbeing for all creatures ever since – including humans.

> "At a fundamental level, I never saw any difference between us and other species; we're all of equal value." He speaks of the hope sometimes expressed by biophiles that humanity will soon wipe itself out, leaving the rest of the biotic community in peace. "I don't think we always get the implications of such a wish: it's actually wishing for far more than anything Hitler ever achieved. Where's the compassion in that? The problem we have now is that humans are designed to deal with the short term and the immediate, and the complex situations we're faced with now are hard for us to understand."

Indeed they are; and they require us to grow up. Peter Pan was a classic Puer, dreaming fantastic dreams but never grounding them in reality. He did become king, but only of the non-existent Neverland. Neverland, like Utopia, is a good place to hold in vision, or to escape to in moments of fantasy. But our own land, Nowland, has real problems which urgently need addressing. In the last section we'll look at ways to engage in the task of growing up, which inevitably involves the loss of treasured old beliefs, as well as gaining expanded new ones.

Idealism remains in the realm of Neverland when it doesn't find a practical outlet. This is a defence (conscious or not) against taking adult, responsible action. The Puer / Puella part of us can procrastinate, seeking all sorts of spiritual and material escape, invoking the importance of doing what 'feels right.' However, when we rely only on our trusted intuition, without establishing real world facts, or when we make choices using our feelings and don't employ critical thinking, when open-mindedness isn't balanced with decisiveness, what 'feels right' can change from one day to the next. Rudderless, we drift on the waves. There are times when drifting is just what we want and need – but as a holiday from, rather than a substitute for, 'real life'. The rudderlessness of a free spirit may seem romantic, but eventually loses its allure. And to others it can look like bewildering inconsistency, or even chaos. Its randomness can be unhelpful and frustrating when trying to plan a campaign, for example, and is downright infuriating for someone who turns up for a meeting to find no-one there because it 'felt right' to do something else. Others' annoyance is keenly felt by the irresponsible but sensitive Puer or Puella: sometimes prompting a flouncing withdrawal, or evoking fiery defensiveness. If we haven't matured sufficiently we can be self-absorbed, and like children, believe everything revolves around us. To work with fellow activists effectively, it helps to develop a middle ground: skilfully navigating and refining the edges between spontaneity and planning.

It's in the Puer / Puella's nature to be candid: authenticity is a core value for most Trembling Warriors. But such openness can cause problems when it shapes our interactions outside our awareness, sometimes making us unnecessarily vulnerable, sometimes alienating others with 'too much information'. The good opinion of others is important to sensitive idealists, but where some will happily tweak the truth to hold on to others' good opinion, others tend to insist on authenticity as a moral standard, and are surprised when they lose that good opinion as a result. In the world of activism it is often necessary to state a glaring though unpopular truth – and naming the elephant in the room often falls to the Puer / Puella. Such a quality is naturally seen as disruptive. In our attempt to serve the greater good by speaking our truth, our inner Child may not anticipate that some will take it personally – even though we might be amongst the first to do so ourselves. With maturity (and mindful practice) comes better judgement to gauge when to speak our truth, and when to hold it close.

Within every Puer / Puella, though, lurks a knowing, even visionary, old man or woman. A 21-year-old client told me, "One of my colleagues said I had an old head on young shoulders, and another said I was the most naïve person he'd ever met – within the space of a few weeks." He was wondering who was right. And of course, both were.

Jenna is an artist in her fifties, raising her daughter alone. She recognises the Puella archetype.

> "It may sound odd, but I've had to reclaim my naïvety. I tried to find my way through the world having had good enough, but perhaps naïve, parenting. In my teens I found out the world wasn't the fairyland I'd been promised, and I became angry and cynical. I rebelled against everything and everyone: raged against the machine. I can still touch into the power of my fury about the system. Punk rock could have been invented for me, but it only made me more angry and bleak. With no soul mentoring, I inevitably got sucked in to various underworlds of drugs, illegal activities, and rampant promiscuity. I got involved in all sorts of crazy scenes; it's hard to believe now I live peacefully as an artist in the wilds of Cumbria. I've had to learn to trust people, to see the best in them, to see beauty, the way I did when I was a little girl. All those lost years! I fear every day that my daughter will get caught up in the bad stuff. I tell myself that if she does, she'll survive it like I did. Hopefully she'll have a better grounding than me, somewhere to put it all and make sense of it. I'm hoping to enrol her on a Wildwise programme next year so she can do the whole walkabout thing properly: in safe hands, physically and spiritually."

Naïvety is a liability, and it is a precious gift. We would do well to honour it by developing as many mature adults in society as possible, who can in turn provide true nurturing eldership for all generations.

Lover

Some Trembling Warriors have a tendency to fall headlong into emotional and sensory love: with men and women, songs and forests, stories and ideas. Enchanted by the Other, they love with great energy and generosity - until the fire of passion burns itself out. Trembling Warriors who have developed enough discernment and discipline might adapt to a new phase of enduring but more mundane loving. But those with a strong streak of Puer or Puella sooner or later grow restless and discontented. Maybe they move on to a new lover, or the ideas of some freshly discovered thinker: whatever breathes oxygen onto their hungry spark. Others can experience quite the opposite: trainee therapist Edwin tells me, "It takes me a long time to get started because I'm looking for the perfect cause/position/ideology to commit to." The underlying values of both, though - what they love and what they abhor - tend to remain as deep and constant embers.

Naturally, mainstream society has a view about fickleness. Many see it as *wrong* to engage wholeheartedly with a cause and then withdraw, to end friendships, romances or working relationships when they grow stale, or to live the nomadic life of the wanderer. Such behaviour is certainly disruptive. But such is the path of some, with all its pros and cons - indeed, from that glorious but challenging journey of hills and valleys, a more emotionally settled life can look flat and colourless. Emotional intuitives thrive on intimacy. What is disconcerting over-familiarity for others, is their essential nourishment.

When you encounter fellow Trembling Warriors, you may feel a spark as energies merge in the space between you. Such synergy may be accompanied by (or mistaken for) sexual attraction, but is more often a meeting of minds, hearts and souls. Even where there is physical attraction, you don't necessarily need to act it out; the soul connection is most significant. What beautiful work might emerge from such a synchronicitous meeting? How might you inspire each other to create and individuate? However, you may need to watch your fiery Puer or Puella here. Your eagerness for intimate connection may not be shared by the other; you may even get a shock to discover they thought you were hoping to seduce them. Worse, you discover you've hurt someone who thought you were feeling your way towards intimacy, when you didn't intend that at all (or sincerely believed that you didn't.)

Less complicated is the Trembling Warrior's love for other-than-human beings. Significant though these relationships often are, there is less anxiety about whether love is requited, and less risk of broken hearts on either side. In nature we can love purely and easily, and we do. A well-grounded biophile has learned to be fascinated by entropy as well as creation: has an animal curiosity about the smell of death and decay as well as honeysuckle and citrus flowers. We love not just Life, but the whole process of Life: a love that guides our morals, and fuels our work.

Trembling Warriors, ardent lovers of Life, feel a responsibility to defend the existence and wellbeing of all. Any psychologically healthy person is drawn to nurture others, but the mature Trembling Warrior loves and serves the whole biosphere. Love-based activism may look the same as purely fear-based activism but it feels very different, springing as it does from concern for others. When we love like this we feel more sorrow than anger about harm to Life; our impulse is generative rather than defensive or retaliatory.

Unlike the erotic love that allures us, this kind of love is self-sacrificing compassionate care, often unconditional, known to the ancient Greeks as *agape*. Such perceptive love enables us to understand intuitively what living beings, human or otherwise, are striving to become, and to assist them in unfolding into becoming. It is sometimes passionate, sometimes very gentle. Many a sensitive idealist is in professional service of others' growth; from our love springs our vocational sense of enabling, our desire to contribute to the greater good. I remember a Swedish man approaching middle-age, sitting in my consulting room and saying urgently, "*I just want to contribute*," desperate to convey a rising, overwhelming urge to vocation that was seeking its channel.

Even with self-esteem in good shape, Trembling Warriors tend to present themselves in a way that's pleasing to others. A lover's warmth toward the world may be variously interpreted as flirtation, sycophancy, naïvety, or subservience. There may be truth in this, but just as often such qualities are projected. Trembling Warriors value warm connection for its own sake; they are no respecters of power and hierarchy; they are often aware of others' intentions (or lies) but choose to overlook them; or they will likely stop being so pleasing the instant their values are compromised.

Trembling Warrior lovers are gentle, and kind: they try to please others not so much because they want to be liked (although that's a welcome bonus) but because *they want others to feel good about themselves*. Others don't - can't - always see that. The currency of compliments has been rendered largely void by the automatic suspicion arising from so much cynical misuse. Too often, compliments are experienced by onlookers (and, sadly, receivers of compliments) as flattery, seduction, manipulation, patronisation, or downright lies – all of which are anathema to the sensitive idealist... although such qualities may well reside in our shadow. Trembling Warriors have a lifelong identity and confidence struggle arising from being misunderstood by those who can't see what motivates us, who inevitably see us through their own lens. Sometimes, though, others provide the uncomfortable but invaluable service of mirroring back to us the aspects of ourselves that we are blind to.

We are told by the cynical that pure altruism can never truly exist: that we always get some form of pay-off from generous-spirited acts. As a friend put it: "I always assumed altruism was supposed to be just one way: if you feel good about it, it's not altruism." But it is: altruism with benefits. Naturally you feel pleased, content, when you have an opportunity to do what you're born for. To castigate yourself for feeling 'smug' misses the point, and colludes with a cynical rejection of generosity. Sometimes, of course, you may make a self-interested decision to help someone: whether to heal your loneliness or low self-esteem, or as a more detached manoeuvre in the interest of personal gain. To question the value of such an act ignores the fact that both parties have gained.

When you give, others may wonder what you're out to get. Today, if you make that very human gesture of offering help, it's often called rescuing – with the implication that you're the needy one. Such an interpretation – that kind acts are motivated solely by self-interest – is understandable in a society where government policies, pervasive marketing, and even the arts, encourage a selfish perspective, attitude and behaviour. 'Do-gooder' and 'people-pleaser' are used as insults, in a culture that focuses only on the irritating and pathological aspects of service. Please don't succumb to feeling embarrassed about, even ashamed of, genuine acts of altruism: doing good, or pleasing people. Or even rescuing people. If you saw someone floundering in the water, would you say to yourself, I won't offer to help, that would just be rescuing? Sometimes people really need someone to dive in beside them and hold them up.

Somewhat bizarrely, in today's society it's an act of courage to reclaim giving as a source of joy, service as an authentic and intrinsic expression of the Trembling Warrior. Disavowal of kindness is tragic, at a time when so many feel lonely, cynical or empty inside. Kindness is somewhere in all of us: witness, for example, the enormous amount of volunteer work carried out not only – in fact, not even usually – by idealists. *Anyone* who shows spontaneous, generous-spirited kindness, even if it is thrown back at them, does the world a great service by keeping altruism alive through love.

Preacher

My great-great-grandfather David Griffith, bardic title Clwydfardd, was a travelling preacher as well as a clockmaker and poet, and co-founder of the Eisteddfod (Welsh arts festival). He was certainly a warrior, and a fiery one at that. If he trembled, it was from the passion of his ethical beliefs. In his biography *Right Man, Right Time*, my father, also David Griffith, told how Clwydfardd walked across the mountains of north Wales to preach in neighbouring villages, and was widely respected by those who walked or rode in from their farms and hamlets to hear him.

Today, the mainstream gets its moral leadership from government, media and celebrities. Most know that such 'leadership' lacks integrity and wisdom, but don't see an alternative. The role of preacher all but vanished from society as people recognised that religious establishments had become corrupt, with religion so often used as a mask for control, war, financial gain and the abuse of children. But that isn't the only reason 'preaching,' has become a defamatory term. A man or woman primarily focused on material gain or personal comfort sees ethics as a form of tyranny, threatening to interfere with their right to profit or pleasure. But without cultural ethics or personal morals, not only do we abandon things like kindness and community that make life worth living; we are able to justify the destruction of the web of life on which we all depend.

Idealists take personal morals very seriously. They can spend hours pondering dilemmas, trying to come to the most ethical decision - whether to end a relationship, or what to choose from a menu - tying themselves in knots trying to do the right thing. They are prone to both moral dilemma (not knowing what is the right thing to do) and moral distress (knowing the right thing to do, but feeling unable to do it). They scrutinise not only their own behaviour, but that of society, and strive to keep leaders honest, responsible, concerned for Life, and acting with integrity. Trembling Warriors attempt to hold a peg in moral standards for everyone else, to stop humanity from sliding all the way to the bottom. We may not always do it well. And even when we are doing it skilfully, it doesn't make us popular: others often experience moral guidance as arrogant, judgmental and smug. However, we don't simply criticise others, for not living up to the same moral standards as ours: more often we criticise others *and* ourselves, for not living up to the standards we think everyone would ideally abide by, for the benefit of all living beings. Activist Deb has a strong 'inner preacher'.

> "Someone called me 'earnest' and I was really irritated. But then I thought, no actually, you're right. I do tend to take everything a bit seriously, including myself. That's why I love my friends who aren't like me: they help me lighten up."

Trembling Warriors are called 'do-gooders' when they challenge behaviours that, although they do harm, are in favour with the mainstream. Hardly anyone would call you a do-gooder for suggesting people shouldn't drink and drive, or shouldn't smack children. Yet both these behaviours have been both common and broadly acceptable in the recent past – as leaving engines running in built-up areas is now, although it poisons pavements and playgrounds.

Despite their ethical focus, idealists of course don't have a monopoly on ethics – everyone has their own personal set of moral standards. For example, some see shopping as ethical behaviour, because it fuels the economy – unlike the Trembling Warrior who cares about the damage caused by 'consumption'. Neither do Trembling Warriors all share the same ethics: some will fight for a low-cost housing development, but not the woodland cut down to build it. Others will risk jail to protect wildlife, but have no moral problem with eating animals. So we can come across as annoyingly sanctimonious, not only to consumerists, but to other biophiles too.

A problem for anyone stepping into a role of moral influencer is an expectation of moral perfection: whether that's others' expectations, or your own. When your activism makes your ethical position public, others feel it's reasonable to judge you on your own standards. And when moral influencers fall short of perfection (as they are bound to do) they are charged with hypocrisy. This leaves hedge-dwellers who aspire to some form of moral leadership with two choices: to hide your own moral failures (such as a secret prejudice, or a plastics transgression) or to own your flaws. The first leads to inner conflict with our core value of authenticity, and the second risks loss of credibility – unless you are part of a collective, where standards are collectively held.

The best you can do is ease up on yourself, recognising and accepting that you are not, and never will be, morally perfect. When we communicate about ethical issues (in fact about anything) in a real way, expressing personal responsibility but not shame, confident in our personal congruence, we're much more likely to be heard than if we accept others' projections of sanctity. It also helps when the emphasis is not on what people *shouldn't* be doing, but what we *can* do to make a difference, why it's important – and why it's not easy.

A long time before Clwydfardd, there were those called to the role of society's conscience. Such a role was respected as much as any other important role in the community, in tribes all over the world. Visionary idealists would have come together with other elders in council to discuss serious matters. When it was their turn to speak, they may have said something like: "I have prayed, and thought deeply about this matter. It appears clearly to me that the situation is thus, and I believe what we as a people should do is this...." Some might agree; others might argue for other interests. But the moral or spiritual leader's voice would be as valid as any other council member, and indeed would often be seen to hold an important truth you brought on behalf of the non-human beings. Differences would be discussed with respect, and eventually resolved. You might thank the warrior for their courage; they might thank you for your vision. But today, you alert your community to the fragility of the web of life, and a large section of the community says, "Fuck off! Who are you to tell me how I should live my life?"

Yet Trembling Warriors still feel the need to speak out, perhaps more insistently than ever, with our vision of how humans are going wrong, and an irrepressible urge to inform our community, so we can all put things right. And it gets us into trouble. One friend, on reading *The Game*, gently mocked me for my 'preacher gene'. And fair enough: it's a strongly worded book. If my work isn't seen, it can be frustrating and disappointing. But when someone calls me out for preaching, or being bossy, or judgmental, it really rankles – because they're qualities I really dislike. I pride myself on my open mind, tolerance, and compassion. How could they see me that way? But when I reflect on how I myself experience being told what to do, it's easy (and humbling) to understand...

Transpersonal psychologist Carl Jung warned against the dangers of projecting all the woundedness on to the patient, and over-identifying with the role of healer. In the same way, the 'preacher' is in danger of projecting all the badness onto the 'congregation', and over-identifying with the role of saint. As long as we bear that in mind, Trembling Warriors are entitled to as much preacher wisdom as we have worked for and attained.

Hermit

Many (though by no means all) Trembling Warriors are by nature introverts: preserving their dreams, keeping something precious in a carefully guarded hut in the forest. Such self-knowledge is useful to come back to when our culture considers extraversion preferable, and even more healthy. Extraverts assume that if you're quiet, there must be something wrong. As Susan Cain explains in her book *Quiet*, they are often (though not always) mistaken. *Repression* of what wants to come through and be expressed can be unhealthy. But holding your energy close and keeping your counsel, listening when you have nothing to say, is not only healthy but wise. Most extraverts would agree wholeheartedly that speaking before thinking can sometimes be regrettable. There are times for both: as Jimi Hendrix said, 'Knowledge talks, wisdom listens'.

Particularly intuitive Trembling Warriors see myriad possibilities, and connections between ideas that others don't see. Add a tendency to introversion, and a dash of self-doubt, and all that depth doesn't go swiftly into words. A friend described her experience.

> "Someone says something that lands with me in a certain way, and I have to think, *what is this?* and roll it round internally to get it, to really let it land. People see my hesitation as not knowing. I can see impatience and then dismissal flickering across their faces as I try to think. Meanwhile the conversation moves on..."

In some situations – such as finding a frog who's fallen into a bucket – a simple assessment is all that's necessary: what needs to happen is clear. But very often, it's vital to explore complexities before a decision is made. Intuitives working with others, for example organising a major protest, may anticipate unforeseen harm to some aspect of the whole, or an indirect compromise of ethics. Then it's incumbent on us to come out of our hut and express what we intuit, as clearly as we can. Slowing the conversation down is really challenging in today's high-speed pressure, and being heard can be truly difficult. An intuitive sense of knowing can't easily be explained, and doesn't hold water for practical or logical types who are looking for proof, or evidence – and fast. So, you have to keep practising: to develop the resilience and authentic presence to have your voice heard, and the language to persuade others of the validity of your vision. Claim your pause for thought. Otherwise you are likely to express what you experience as vast, complex, and significant in a few brushstroke words: the best you can manage at the time. Those around you may simply see you as wilfully obscure, mysterious or superior – or just random. Someone will be thinking, if not asking, "Where did *that* come from?"

Introverted Trembling Warriors are necessarily reclusive at times. We may like the *idea* of collaboration, team work and close-knit community. But the reality is somewhat different: we can soon find we've had enough of extraverting, and our inner hermit has us head for our hut in the woods. Done mindfully, this is very healthy: silence is *essential* if you are not to lose sight of what really matters. Withdrawing from mainstream society can help you stay uninfected by psychological manipulation and despair; as mythologist and story-teller Martin Shaw says, "If all you do is stare into hell, you will become ashes." If you often withdraw to the hut, it might be helpful to discern between a calling to solitude and your own fear; to find your right balance between precious freedom and integration with society. All hermits, however, should re-enter society at times: not only to stay informed, but to bring that purer (less infected) perspective back into the flow of humanity, where it is very much needed. Also, it's important not to alienate yourself from others and start to believe you're the only one who sees the truth, the only one trying to bring about change. That can create a sense that you are all alone, fighting against everyone around you, which leads to disillusionment, depletion and disengagement.

Sensitive idealists are prone to isolation for several reasons. Perhaps you gently dismiss overtures of friendship from those you don't think share your values, leaving them feeling 'judged and found wanting'. You may not like the *thought* of impacting on others in this way, and indeed may be unaware that you do. But you dislike inauthentic friendships more. And with those you do admire (and perhaps idealise), you might - rightly or wrongly - imagine yourself slighted by them, and withdraw: often with a dramatic gesture, burning bridges behind you. Even with beloved friends, you may be prone to disappearing and lying low: not picking up messages, declining invitations. You may need solitude for creativity or replenishment; maybe you feel bruised by the world, and need to heal. A friendship needs a certain age and depth to withstand such periods; otherwise people can assume you're not interested in them, and drop the acquaintance. However, there are those who find such evasiveness intriguing and alluring, and persist.

Sadly, tender idealists are susceptible to depression, or at least periods of melancholy. Depression has complex causes, forms and cures. Some therapists insist that it always indicates underlying anger. Whilst suppressed anger is a common theme in depression, such a finite diagnosis can be dangerously misleading. For example, for many with an idealistic temperament, contributing to wellbeing is our life blood. When we are not engaged by some form of meaningful work, we are prone to sinking into a swamp. Without a clear purpose, an experience of contributing, you may begin to wonder what your life is for. Furthermore, tenderness renders some liable to being diminished by rejection or criticism. And if that wasn't enough for Trembling Warriors, melancholy is an inevitable aspect of life in the 21st century. With the ideals we cherish so severely undermined, and threatened with such force and on such a scale, it's all too easy to drop into a dark cave. Green activist Paula tells a story that will be all too familiar to some.

> "This depression has several roots. There's the stark and unavoidable environmental dragon of man-made climate change and its associated suffering for both humankind and biodiversity and hence life on Earth.

> Do any problems get bigger than that? Plus, there are the very human changes which occur, with hormones taking me on unprecedented rides just as parents are in their twilight years and needing a lot of support. And my two daughters had grown up and flown the nest, full of young adult joy – and my heart aches at the thought of what they will face."

We'll come back to Paula in the last section to find how she addressed her depression.

The wisdom of the soul knows when you need some time in a dark cave, and pulls you down. Such times usually pass, although it can feel like they never will. But with too much solitude, your fire can't thrive. You may like the *idea* of a cloistered, peaceful life, but sooner or later your energy returns and you grow restless, pricking your ears as you smell the battle on the wind.

Woodcock

Woodcocks have a special skill. Their unique eyes giving them 360-degree vision, they can see all around without moving. Some Trembling Warriors naturally see all sides, too. Activists with definite opinions are more like owls with forward-facing eyes. They know exactly what they're trying to achieve, and generally have the discipline to fulfil their commitments to themselves and others. This, combined with great practicality, gives a clear and obvious sense of what is 'right' and what is 'wrong'. These owls may have to make a conscious effort to look all around them – to understand divergent worldviews.

A valuable gift Woodcocks can bring to the frontline is readiness to acknowledge and consider another's perspective, even when it differs considerably from their own. When this is combined with a healthy emotional life, empathetic understanding is added to the mix. All this can be used in negotiations, whether in political or ground-based activism, without having to *agree*. An ability to acknowledge the complexity of things can help immensely, as you engage with those who might be persuaded to act for Life instead of colluding with destruction.

Activists with all-round vision have a natural awareness of complexity. The more direct owl types tend to see the world in a more black and white, linear way. For things like dealing with frogs in buckets, remembering facts, and making quick decisions, a more simplistic view can be really useful – and doesn't come easily to those of us who haven't developed their practical or decisive faculties. But not everything is simple. As Jean Boulton writes in *Embracing Complexity*, 'Wishing the world was predictable and controllable does not make it so, and might make us disregard what is actually happening.'

Willingness to see all sides, though, comes with its drawbacks (at least for humans, if not woodcocks). As one idealist put it, "Seeing both sides of the story weakens my stance, with someone who isn't prepared to see mine." And another: "I find I end up watering down what I want to say. I imagine all the critical voices and I tone it down, making sure I acknowledge the other side for balance. I don't want anyone thinking I'm naïve, or that I don't understand where other people are coming from."

A lot of people like certainty (or what's actually an illusion of certainty). It makes them feel they're in safe, parental hands they can trust. That's why Conservatives preached their 'strong and stable' message, but I wonder: did they believe it themselves?

Some idealists can be so open-minded that they procrastinate endlessly. Reluctant activists might never move forward with anything, dreading and putting off the inevitable closing of other possible doors. They may keep making changes: to the text of a petition, plans for an event, or the aim of a campaign. They may offer to do something, and then fail to follow through. Such behaviour is especially chronic when a strong preference for keeping options open is combined with a butterfly mind that darts around to new ideas. Needless to say, this can be incredibly frustrating to others on our team, who would love us to stretch ourselves a bit and develop some discipline and certainty. Eleanor Roosevelt had wise words about congruence and adherence.

> "The standards by which you live must be your own standards, your own values, your own convictions in regard to what is right and wrong, what is true and false, what is important and what is trivial. When you adopt the standards and the values of someone else or a community or a pressure group, you surrender your own integrity. You become, to the extent of your surrender, less of a human being."

The only way any of us can acquire and develop our own standards and values is by reference to others. As teenagers, we 'try on' the various personae we come across, wearing them for a while to see if they fit. One task of maturing is to gradually pare away that which doesn't align with our deeply held values.

Seeing all sides helps with the important recognition that each activist has their own personal priorities. If someone is dedicated to farm animal welfare but doesn't support an anti-hunting campaign, it doesn't mean they don't love animals: it means they're giving their time and energy to the issue which speaks to them most. A family who campaign against deportations but don't attend a fundraiser aren't necessarily hypocritical: they're probably making informed decisions and choosing their compromises, as we all must. None of us is perfect - though most idealists would like to be. Accepting, embracing and encouraging others' priorities (and therefore their contribution to the greater good), can reduce in-fighting, stress and suspicion amongst activists. And that creates easier, more enjoyable relationships, freeing up energy for the battles that actually matter. Divided, we fall.

I wrote in the Introduction how my nine-year-old self vowed never to travel on roads again, a vow that was soon broken, like many other vows since. You may recognise this pattern... painfully moved by a video showing footage of farm animals being mistreated, you may vow never to eat meat again - until a host serves chicken curry, or your body craves meat because you have your period, or simply because you fancy a bacon roll. Such a way of being is natural if your intuition has you leap to new ideas, and you like to keep your options open. Your conscience, however, probably gives you a hard time for behaving in ways not congruent with your values This can lead to inner conflict, stress and anxiety. And others, quite understandably, accuse you of hypocrisy. Those with well-developed discipline (who are excellent at keeping vows) can't understand why you should believe in a certain principle, and then not live it wholeheartedly yourself. You'll likely be sensitive to this criticism, valid though it is: woodcocks are very good at picking up threats in their environment. Artist Jenna knows her discipline could do with some strengthening:

> "I feel at the time I really want to commit to something, and then I don't: I make myself an excuse. We can be very good at justifying our decisions. When I have to fulfil obligations to others, be disciplined, I can resent that.

> There is some joy in kicking over the traces, but guilt always follows it: 'Now look what I've done!'

The Puer or Puella in us chafes at boundaries and limits, viewing restrictions as intolerable. Paradoxically, though, some restrictions are necessary for our emotional growth.

If your activism is at all public, you'll find yourself pulled in all directions: everyone will have an opinion on what you should or shouldn't do. Whether it's a family member or a famous guru doesn't matter: sift through it all and check in with your soul to find what feels right, at the deepest and truest level. Then call on, or develop, some closure, and ditch the rest. And if that feels too absolute, at least park it for now...

Humility

Maria Popova, who somehow finds time to produce the rich weekly digest of wisdom that is *Brainpickings*, has studied many of our finest writers on the topic of humility and creativity.

> 'There is a fine but firm line between critical thinking and cynical complaint. To cross it is to exile ourselves from the land of active reason and enter a limbo of resigned inaction. But cross it we do, perhaps nowhere more readily than in our capacity for merciless self-criticism. We tend to go far beyond the self-corrective lucidity necessary for improving our shortcomings, instead berating and belittling ourselves for our foibles with a special kind of masochism.'

Maria could be writing this especially for the Trembling Warriors who are all too prone to self-denigration. Vocal inner critics are, like the hierarchical institutions we so resent, a form of tyranny: always imposing standards we can't reach. We don't like being ruled through fear, but sometimes we do it to ourselves. I meet plenty of Trembling Warriors who give themselves a hard time for what they see as their own hypocrisy, failure, or general worthlessness. If sensitive souls don't undertake the long, slow, and often costly work of rebuilding their sense of self-worth, they are forever berating themselves; forever apologising to others.

As we've seen, failure to adhere to ideals can spawn worries about hypocrisy, and sleepless nights. When that happens, you're playing the Avoider avatar described in *The Game*. There are two healthy ways out of this fix. You can either acknowledge you screwed up and develop your discipline, enabling you to keep to your personal best – or, you can accept that you looked away from that teenager sleeping in a shop door, or that you accepted the plastic bag, and forgive yourself: one such decision doesn't make you 'a bad person', and you can always engage more mindful choice-making next time. But agonising without action or decision is untenable; it doesn't serve anyone or anything.

Sincere and pure eagerness to please is delightful. Combined with wobbly self-esteem, it can undermine what we're trying to achieve in the world. Trembling Warriors can downplay themselves, almost to the point of disappearing. They lurk on social media, keep quiet in meetings; apologise for their views, their sensitivity, their presence, for speaking their truth, and even for their very existence. Concerned not to appear 'holier than thou', some swing too far the other way with disclaimers: constantly reminding themselves and everyone else about their own hypocrisy, fallibility and part in the destruction. So as to make themselves palatable, many Trembling Warriors pretend be more immoral than they actually are. In these crucial times, we need to stop over-apologising for defending Life. Over-apologising negates the importance and validity of who you are and what you do, weakening your agency in an already cynical mainstream that admires and expects confidence and certainty in its leaders. If you disavow the validity of your work in the world, what is left to you?

When you apologise unnecessarily, speak hesitantly, smile ingratiatingly, or undersell yourself, you signal like a lighthouse: 'I have nothing of worth to say'. When you use words, voice or gestures which make you smaller, you are (albeit unconsciously) being a submissive animal. When dogs crouch down, look away, or roll over, they're expressing, *Don't hurt me: I'm not worthy, I'm low-status, I'm small. I'm not a threat.* Pragmatic activist Sarah told me how frustrated she was when fellow protestors kept hopping onto the pavement with their banners, saying they didn't want to hold people up. "That's the whole point!" she said in exasperation.

Polite or diffident behaviour may keep us safe from the reprisals a child might fear, but as mature adults we have every right to confidently own our unique niche. Sometimes we just need to catch up with that fact, challenging and uncomfortable though this spurt of growth may be. We all have responsibilities, and they are easier to meet when we're able to fully own our activist role, whatever form it takes. (We'll look at some different forms in the next section.)

Those struggling with an impoverished or even starving sense of self-worth may (again unconsciously) put themselves down in the hope that others will rescue them, by telling them how good they are. Expressions of authentic gratitude and affirmation are intrinsically beautiful and useful: nourishing and affirming for both parties, and powerful encouragers of bold work. But praise becomes unhealthy when it's inauthentic, given to flatter or manipulate, or when the one receiving praise is (and stays) stays dependent on it for their sense of worth. Counsellor Anne sees a lot of self-criticism in her consulting room.

> "We only *think* we're not worthy: at the core of things, it's not true. Diffidence isn't a deliberate lie. But if you were to believe in your own power, then what might be expected of you? If you claim your self-worth, and do something out there in the world, can you cope with the competition, the jealousy, and the projections? If you put yourself forward for something, are you setting yourself up for a fall if you can't fulfil it? You're risking humiliation, which takes you straight back to diffidence. It's a form of self-protection, and one of the reasons we like it in others is that it's non-threatening."

Trembling Warriors need to cultivate *humility* rather than *apology*. Humility has a subtly different, and much more powerful, quality. True humility is unselfconscious. It is what it is; no apologies (or compensatory over-inflations) are needed. Of course not all Trembling Warriors suffer from low self-worth: indeed, many have a quiet sense of being 'good enough' that they either grew up with, or have learned. They may know themselves unaccepted by the mainstream, but they're good enough for themselves and those around them, and that's sufficient. Even with self-esteem in good shape, introverted idealists tend to hold back from talking about what they know and what they've done. This is often because they don't want anyone to feel deskilled or diminished by their 'superior' knowledge. We have consideration because we know what being diminished feels like, and we don't want to do it to others. After all, we're all about helping people grow, not making them feel smaller. Often, though, our projected care is unwarranted: most people are more likely to be interested in our experience and knowledge than threatened by it.

Diffidence, of course, has its grandiose shadow side. Some idealists, particularly the young ones (or the eternally young Puer or Puella), secretly suspect that they *are* in some way special - and may feel guilty or nervous about entertaining such an idea. The notion of being 'special' raises the twin spectres of delusion and responsibility. We can deal with the first by reminding ourselves that *everyone* is special. Each person has a particular and essential gift to bring forward: the purpose we were born to fulfil. The Trembling Warrior's speciality is acting as the eco-conscience of society, interceding between humanity and the rest of the living world. It *is* a special role, and privileged. So is the role of the food grower, without whom we would all starve. I re-emphasise the parity to avoid any intimation of *special* specialness - which may be hard to accept for those who strongly identify with the Puer / Puella archetype. Our specialness only become *especially* special in our secret dreams if it's been repressed: when we welcome it in, it loses some of its shadowy potency.

The responsibility that goes with your speciality is less easily dismissed. We are each here to perform a particular role, and each of us has at least one unique gift. Our first responsibility is to discover what our gift is. Then we must find how to deliver it.

Maverick

Trembling Warriors are often told they're *different.* Essentially non-conformist, they see connections others don't see, and cleave to values others don't understand. They 'come out with strange things'; they're seen as eccentric. They may be labelled as simply dyslexic, or autistic; indeed, many of today's Earth Warriors have an autism diagnosis, as Steve Silberman explains in *Neurotribes.* Others are diagnosed with a minor mental illness such Attention Deficit Disorder, or (scarily) 'Oppositional Defiant Disorder' for those who don't conform. A Washington Post article remarked that if Mozart were alive today, he'd be diagnosed with ADHD and 'medicated into barren normality.' However, nonconformity is probably the healthiest response to today's dominant paradigm. As Krishnamurti said, "It is no measure of health to be well adjusted to a profoundly sick society."

Mavericks are like weeds that thrive wherever they seeded, and bloom wherever they grow, cheerfully refusing to conform to the straight lines and strict cultivars of regimented gardens. Wild and spontaneous, they appear, do their beautiful and fecund thing, and then either stay around or vanish forever. The controlling gardener, nervous about such exuberance, fights back with trowels, poisons and plastic double-gloving. Mavericks are like spirited pigs who occasionally spot an opportunity for escape from the grim journey between their cramped, stinking pens and the sterile concrete ramp of the slaughterhouse. Cavorting away across the countryside, they lead determined officials a merry dance, enjoying their freedom and foraging, until they're captured.

It's not that mavericks play by their own rules: rather, they trample the rulebook (or Bible, or curriculum, or policy) into the mud, leaving it to slowly compost; or they make origami birds of it, or confetti that they scatter playfully on the warm south wind. Subversive Trembling Warriors are guided primarily by their own strong internal values: what feels right, and what feels true. The

Puer / Puella, as we've seen, can have us innocently ask piercing, exposing questions, or make observations that throw a spotlight on the consensually unspoken – which can contribute to being seen as the outsider; the disruptor. It's not a popular role, but it's a vital one if 'developed' society is to be woken from its collusion with the destruction of Life.

No wonder the maverick Trembling Warrior looks odd to the mainstream. As Nietzsche put it: 'Those who were seen dancing were thought to be insane by those who could not hear the music.' Trembling Warriors often *are* a little unconventional, and there's no point pretending otherwise. If you are 'different', you may as well fully inhabit your differentness: celebrate it, rather than carry it shamefully, as if you were more flawed than anybody else. Finding other mavericks helps with this greatly. Men on the edge are often seen as mysterious lone wolves, whereas women on the edge are somehow more easily diminished, or dismissed as crazy witches. But whatever your gender, if you are blessed with enough confidence and charisma to truly inhabit a peripheral place, you are blessed indeed.

Such independence of spirit, of course, has its shadow. Mature rebellion requires constructive alternatives to the system. Rebellion fuelled by personal hurts is a furious but immature response to *any* kind of authority, ego-centric (focusing on the self) rather than eco-centric (with attention to the whole biosphere). Witness Trump, a maverick if ever there was one. An eco-centric maverick *can* submit willingly to authority – but only that of an authentic leader with integrity. Other attempts at 'managing' us will only evoke our Trembling Warrior fire. Naturally this leads to trouble in the conventional workplace. Trembling Warriors *can't* simply do as we're told, unless we're offered a good reason. If instructions offend our sense of what's right, we're more likely to do what's right than follow the instructions. It's easy to see why some organisations use psychological tests to help weed out mavericks at the interview stage. Despite the rhetoric, what most companies want from the vast majority of their employees is obedience and compliance. They think they want creativity, but they think they can get it conditionally, subject to obedience first. And when they get creativity, they realise they've also got risk, and it makes them nervous: 'We didn't mean *that*!'.

The maverick shows up in the archetype of the Fool, whose role is to 'subvert prevailing orthodoxy and orthopraxis in order to point to the truth which lies beyond immediate conformity.' Awareness and knowledge of the Fool archetype that we embody can help us to carry it with confidence and authority, rather than shame. And how we show up determines to a large extent whether we're taken seriously, or dismissed.

Hens who are different from the others are often pecked to death, and humans who are noticeably different also get a hard time. When we know we're counter-current by nature, it's sometimes easier to camouflage ourselves, and blend in. Paul is an IT expert and writer.

> "I've always felt passionate about politics, social justice and so on, yet learnt from a young age that I was very non-conforming and it was safer to keep my views to myself. My thinking around various things has led me to be radical and non-conformist on most subjects, yet I feel uncomfortable with drawing attention to myself as an outsider. For example, I have always like 'alternative' music and so on, but tended to dress rather unremarkably."

Some Trembling Warriors strive to create a life in which they can stay relatively free of consumer trends, unjust company policies, laws and regulations - in fact anything that conforming to would flout their most deeply values. But there are also many things worth conforming to. For example, I sing in a choir. To sing with the others effectively, I have to relinquish my ego and become part of the greater whole, take guidance from others. The same is true when we want to accomplish anything worthwhile in the world. Then, conforming to the norms of those around us isn't just sensible: it's crucial. That's why the company we choose – the peer group that dictates our norms – is so important.

Thirty-nine-year-old Henry spoke of his desire to be an activist by refusing to capitulate: he dreamed of travelling on foot with a pony, finding itinerant work. "But I'm afraid of where I'll land," he said. On one hand he passionately didn't want to collude with the mainstream; on the other hand, he was afraid his family would judge him careless, and possibly reject him, if he did what his heart was urging him to do. Ironically, self-doubt kept him from being the hedge-dweller he longed to be.

A mature Trembling Warrior knows when to conform and when to rebel, using well-developed intuition and thinking to adopt the most appropriate strategy for the most eco-centric outcome. It might involve 'playing the game': going along with mainstream administrative systems in order to learn, or to build a network of connections, or to influence from within.

Early in 2019, someone attempted to discredit new young American senator Alexandria Ocasio-Cortez, by showing a 2010 video of her dancing on a college roof. Twitter reaction showed that more and more people can hear Nietzsche's music; that maybe a dancing congresswoman isn't so eccentric after all, but actually offers a vision of what leadership could look like in a healthier, more joyful future.

Visionary

Idealists who are both visionary *and* humble may be reluctant to use the first word about themselves, for fear of sounding pretentious. Yet visioning need be no more grand than nurturing, strategising, or organising. Anyone who performs their work in a highly skilled, exemplary way is entitled to a bit of pomposity. We all experience a rollercoaster of achievement and humility, and if all goes well, an underlying trajectory of growth in skill. Whatever your role, you were born with the fundamental aptitude for it. Then it's up to you to recognise your gift; then learn it, develop it and refine it. The Trembling Warrior visionary's contribution to activism is threefold:

- To perceive the nature of relationships (between heart and mind, body and soul; or between human beings; humanity and other beings, across species, and in the complex, fragile, web of life on Earth, and perhaps beyond

- To perceive stories: a person's story, a people's story; the story of a relationship, a species, a place, or a planet; and to sense into the trajectory of a story: the journey that has led thus far, and possible paths leading forwards

- To sense what is healthful and what is harming, and to know oneself strongly committed to what is healthful; to discern what is needed to bring about a healthful future; to dream that future into being; and to express insights in some form.

Although society has forgotten how to value or reward such a role, this is what a visionary's Job Description might look like. Any role needs clear definition, and anyone embodying a role needs the right support and conditions to become skilled at it, in order to deploy it alongside others' work.

'Visionary', for our purposes, includes the ability to perceive the numinous: what psychologist Jerome Bernstein calls the 'transrational' - that which is beyond understanding through reason alone. Many gentle idealists have never quite lost their wonder at the world: their belief in magic, in talking animals, and in the realness of dreams. Some say we haven't quite grown up. We might respond that we are still able to perceive what most have lost the ability to see, pointing out that the such phenomena are not 'super'-natural, but simply natural. In ancient times when magic, dreams and the voices of animals were a normal part of daily life, visionaries were those who could 'see' or foresee extraordinary events. They would have been respected and listened to; today the transrational is ridiculed. So we keep it quiet, or more often suppress and ignore it, in a mainstream that doesn't believe in, and is rather afraid of, magic. (By magic, I mean what is termed 'supernatural' because we don't yet have a rational explanation for it.) Awareness of the transrational gives us glimpses of the great energy/matter/consciousness flow of (and perhaps beyond) the universe. It has been called Mind-fire by the Stoics, and Nature by Marcus Aurelius; The Mystery by Bill Plotkin, the Holoflow by holistic scientist Brian Goodwin; others call it the Source. Some, including visionary and maverick scientist Rupert Sheldrake, call it 'God'.

The visionary manifests in many ways: empath Anna Breytenbach, who can discern what animals are feeling and expressing; powerful writer and speaker Mac Macartney, who senses the voices of ancient peoples; mythologist Martin Shaw, who raises his eyes and sees nature spirits all around. There are those who have a rich, creative imagination, those who remember former lives, those who can divine water, and those who read signs in the stars. Psychologist Jerome Bernstein's description of 'Borderlanders' (those who feel non-human pain) will resonate with many a Trembling Warrior.

> 'Borderland people personally experience, and must live out, the split from nature on which the western ego, as we know it, has been built. They feel (not feel *about*) the extinction of species; they feel (not feel about) the plight of animals *who* are no longer permitted to live by their own instincts, and *who* survive only in domesticated states to be used as pets or food. Such people are highly intuitive. Many, if not most, are psychic to some degree, whether they know it or not. They are deeply feeling, sometimes to such a degree that they find themselves in profound feeling states that seem irrational to them. Virtually all of them are highly sensitive on a bodily level. They experience the rape of the land in their bodies; they psychically, and sometimes physically, gasp at the poisoning of the atmosphere.'

(Borderlanders will understand why I have replaced Bernstein's 'that' and 'which' with *who*.)

A more-than-average number of Borderlanders suffer from mental health disturbances, often originating in or exacerbated by the pain of the world in these times, as well as an alienating sense of being *seen* as mentally ill by society (and by some therapists). Even healthy Borderlanders can be seen as crazy if they express their experience - and so most stay quiet about it. It's likely that before the western ego separated itself from nature in order to exploit it, transrational experiences were an unquestioned part of life. However, Bernstein reports that such experiences are rising once more. He believes that through visionaries, humanity is trying to reconnect itself with nature, spirit, and soul.

Perhaps everyone has a visionary aspect they can develop if they choose, but in a predominantly rational person, or society, it generally lies latent or is actively suppressed. To anyone with a strong preference for facts and an under-developed imagination, it absolutely matters whether transrational experiences are real. If they can be scientifically proven, so much the better. Any discussion about what 'real' actually means will likely be met with derision. However, for those with strong intuition, 'real' is a somewhat meaningless concept that can easily be suspended. Reality, of course, is highly subjective anyway: one person's transrational experience can be a bit too 'out there' for the next person. Maybe we can't hear the music that crazy woman is dancing to, but who can say whether it's real? Many things previously considered 'out there', such as animal sentience, are now widely accepted. So although we may not share others' visions, we do them respectful service when we hold them in potential as possibilities. I've seen clients totally thrown off the scent of their dreams by a stern, rational, internal or external voice that comes along and says "You are being unrealistic." When they capitulate to that unhelpful critical voice, they are severed from their inner wisdom and so lose their path. Sometimes we all need help discerning between ego-centric personal projections, and the eco-centric, numinous truth.

Transrational experiences can come via plant-based substances such as salvia, ahayuasca, or synthetic chemicals like LSD. But it is also possible to access a transcendent state through meditation. Or, you may notice you're entering a sacred, liminal space as you walk into a forest – particularly if you do so with ritual intention. Sometimes spirit just takes you by surprise: there it is. Other times, you can go seeking numinous experiences but the mundane stays firmly in place, refusing to shift, not allowing you to see beyond the thin but opaque veil that screens the otherworld (some might say the real world) as we go about our daily ego-centric lives.

The more visionary someone is, the more weird they appear to the mainstream – which can understandably discourage the visionary's desire to engage in public discourse. As we've seen, those who inhabit a rich internal realm of ideas can find it hard to have their voices heard: the complexity of their inner vision isn't easy to get into words; especially the quick, neat soundbites expected today. Furthermore, a seeming ability to see into a dark future is easily dismissed as doom-mongering, by those with an interest in preserving the status quo either through fear of change, or a desire to hang on to power and wealth that's dependent on today's economic model. So the visionary is often medicated, incarcerated, or simply ignored - even when they are well, and have something important to say. However, in a society that marginalises innate visionaries, it's sadly all too common for them to lack the wise guidance necessary to live well with their gifts, and they struggle to be in the world. Sometimes they choose to leave it.

The visionary who hasn't yet fully matured may suffer from a lack of financial awareness, or be irresponsible in taking care of physical needs: their own, and other beings in their care. They may have a vision but nowhere to take it, so what actually needs to happen in the world stays forever in the realm of dreams. Bill Plotkin writes in *Soulcraft* that spirituality 'makes possible the experience and expression of unconditional love, perennial wisdom, and healing power.' But unless it's grounded by earthy soul, we might seek to pretend environmental or societal crises aren't happening, don't matter, or will somehow be alright. Floating into the ether of ungrounded spirituality is a way of escaping responsibility. It's an understandable defence from almost unbearable pain or despair, which we may engage without deciding to, or even knowing we have. But once we're aware of it, we can choose to bring ourselves back down to Earth.

Always ready to fall in love with people and ideas, Trembling Warriors can be seduced by false prophets, and purveyors of snake oil. They can conjure universal truths and messages out of their own very personal (and not always healthy) fears and fantasies. They may feel like turning their backs on what story-teller Martin Shaw often calls 'the rinky-dink world'. But as J. K. Rowling had Percy Weasley say: "Wizards should have a thorough understanding of the non-magical community, particularly if they're thinking of working in close contact with them".

Rich imagination, which has been suppressed in a military-industrial world, is absolutely vital to our future, and that of most of Life as it currently exists. Industrialised humanity has become so mired in its destructive track, that only the talons of beautiful, powerful dreams can pull us free. It's of great importance that we keep our connection with the numinous alive. Visionaries and dreamers have been suppressed in waves ever since the rational mind split away from the rest - but today, on behalf of humanity, we hold what could be the last spark of life. We have a responsibility to tend and develop it in ourselves and each other: to learn to trust it. And we must do all this despite pressure from the mainstream, which can be very hard if you're isolated. In the last section we'll look at ways of nourishing and replenishing the magic.

A Trembling Warrior's Garden

There's a patch of land, a garden that's running wild. It isn't mine. This patch of land will outlast me, just as it's outlasted everyone else who's laid claim to it. But I find myself in the position of being a custodian of it, for the time being. I can explore it, sit quietly in it, gaze up at the trees, and plant things. I can discover the soil, and the soul of it. Sometimes I get the feeling that I belong to this patch of land, rather than the other way round. It has quietly taken hold of me.

It seems wild but it isn't. It was once cultivated and domesticated and is now relaxing, being more spontaneous. Plants and animals that weren't welcome before are coming back. The trees are huge and their branches intertwine. Overgrown bushes and brambles obscure quite how far back the garden goes. Behind the shed, which is slowly surrendering to the weight of a tree leaning on its roof, is a den of foxes. At night, I hear their voices: to my ears, a disembodied, eerie shrieking. I wonder what they are doing, out there in the dark. In the daylight, I discover the evidence of their play. Plastic bags, a squeaky ball, odd shoes. They are scattered on the "lawn", which is a green carpet of weeds. Or at least, I used to think they were weeds; now I realise I don't know what they are. When I dig into the soil, I discover that, far from being solid local clay, it is rich and loamy. It's well populated by earthworms, quietly digesting their way around beneath the surface. Someone must have added compost once. As I plunge my hands into the soil, I'm uncovering the memories of past gardens. There are other people's dreams here, laid down in layers, over years. And before that, fields. And before that, trees. And before that...

So what do I want my relationship with this place to be? Do I want to dominate it, imposing form and structure, and tolerate the frustration of its rebellions? Or do I want to let it slide into increasing wildness, letting the brambles become a barrier to human entry? I long to find a path in between. A forest garden. Not exactly wild, but not domesticated either. I long to find coexistence, where everything can be noticed and considered, including my own human needs for solace and vegetables. The garden could offer sustenance in so many ways, to so many beings. I wonder, is this kind of coexistence possible? And by coexistence, I don't mean living side by side, respectfully separate, parallel lives. That's impossible. I mean tolerating, sharing, communicating, paying attention to, respecting, trusting, appreciating and belonging with.

I want to change the way we think about our relationships with the other than human world. And I believe that's inextricably entangled with changing our relationships with each other, and with ourselves. I believe there is a profound connection between the mental health crises of our age - feelings of anxiety, depression, impotence, rage and despair - and a loss of connection to the land we live on, the air we breathe and the other beings we share this earth with. It seems like so little, to think about a garden as a place where people and other beings can practice coexisting. But perhaps doing something little is better than doing nothing...

Helen Allman

PART TWO

Realms of Activism

This section is an invitation to explore fourteen forms of activism: to 'try them on'; to sense into what fits, what doesn't, and what you might grow into. I'll refer back to the qualities described in the last section. Awareness of different personalities also helps throw light on the sort of activism that is right for you, rather than being overly influenced by others' preferences: we can all benefit from stretching into our less preferred ways of being at times, but doing so for too long, as we will see, can cause great stress. And if you prefer not to have a psychometric test determine your actions, simply notice where your attention is truly drawn to, and how it wants to manifest itself.

Sixty-six-year-old Anna Lunk is a seasoned campaigner who has learned what forms of activism work best for her: activities she enjoys, and that draw on her innate skills – and excite her energy. For her, activism and pleasure are perfectly compatible.

> "I've always been passionate about sustainable, affordable housing, and I'm also very interested in the history and work of the Dartington Trust, who own a lot of the land likely to be developed in the village. So, I co-chair the local Neighbourhood Plan, and I enjoyed organising a housing conference at Dartington Hall. Over the years I've found that I'm best suited to organising one-off events with a clear purpose and outcomes. I also enjoy meetings: I think I'm good at summarising arguments and pushing things towards positive outcomes. What I'm

> not good at is detailed reading of long planning documents, understanding the detail of legislation, or reading anything longer than an email on the internet."

Long-term activist Larch Maxey advises those who are drawn to stand up for Life but don't know how, to start with small steps: even just reading an article or watching a short film the issues that speak to you most, and noticing what impulses arise. "Every journey has a first step, and no matter how long we've been activists, we're all on a journey. If we're open enough, we go on deepening that journey, opening our hearts more, and increasing our capacity to be of service." If you're confused about how things are playing out in the world, not sure who to believe or what to do, Larch recommends taking time out every day from the busyness of life to 'listen to the heart': to reflect on what's important to you; to get in touch with, and become clear about, your values, ethics and principles. You may then find you instinctively know where to start looking for ways you can protect what you love.

My personal experience hasn't been of deciding what my 'soul work' is: more one of noticing. When I look back at the books I've written, and my work with clients, they all basically say, 'Humans are hurting the Earth and ourselves, and you have a unique role to play in turning that round.' That's the theme I keep coming back to: what seems to want to be expressed through me. My path will no doubt continue to adapt and evolve, but I can't imagine it putting me down and setting me free.

What is your life's work trying to say, in a sentence or a phrase? Don't worry if you don't have answer to that yet. Psychologist and vision quest leader Bill Plotkin writes fully and generously in all his books about how we can discover the truth of our work. I don't suggest that you accept *all* of his ideas (or anyone's, including mine) as fact, or dogma to be adhered to. But he offers much wisdom for finding your path.

Nearly seventy years ago, John Steinbeck wrote in his novel *East of Eden*: 'There are monstrous changes taking place in the world, forces shaping a future whose face we do not know. Some of these forces seem evil to us, perhaps not in themselves but because their tendency is to eliminate other things we hold good.... at such a time it seems natural and good to me to ask myself these questions. What do I believe in? What must I fight for and what must I fight against?' His grasp of humanity's trajectory was visionary; we now begin to see clearly the face of the future he saw unfolding. I often use a version of his questions with clients.

Your way of contributing will adapt and evolve, so watch your energy closely, developing a sense of when to step forward and when to withdraw. As long as you are following your inner wisdom, there's no need for over-analysis. Your whole organism, body and psyche, knows what is needed – both for you, and for the greater good.

Whatever you do, do it as kindly and gently as you can whilst still being effective. There may be times when you need to take physical risks, and to speak furiously, but use force only when it is necessary, and not simply to vent your rage. The stronger your force, the more it emphasises an 'Othering' dynamic of 'us and them', maintaining a sense of opposition. It also creates something to push back against. Opposing is not the same as opposition. Use your force, but use it wisely; use it discerningly.

Skeena Rathor of Extinction Rebellion describes how the term 'activating' arose as an alternative to 'activism', in a meeting hosted by the Politics Kitchen in Stroud.

> 'As an activator I imagine us listening more deeply for what the need is - in order to activate responses that are primarily about connection rather than orientated in what we think is needed. As an activist we think we 'know what the world needs' what 'justice' means; what is right and wrong. Often, we have decided on the necessary action long before it reaches the zone of effect. As an activator we are in a constantly unfolding or emerging relationship, we are fluid and free of assumption, attachment and expectation. As an activist we seek to; push, campaign, lobby, persuade, protest

> and protect. All of these have virtue and value. As an activator we also speak the truth of our needs, we are committed to deep listening and learning, we put relationship first, we co-create, we do what is most beautiful and we act from love - to activate resonance, to activate alignment, to activate our deepest self, to activate the essence of each other. Activism was an evolutionary step for human kind and I believe that activating will be another step forward. To activate, you are liberating the conversation or specific action. You are energising the interdependent aspects of the issue.'

We'll start at the sharp end with some recognised forms of activism, and then move on to ways you can activate within dominant paradigm, even when it is sometimes uncomfortable – which, after all, defines a Trembling Warrior.

Notice as you read: what draws you? What skills do you bring, or not bring? What do you love? What do you recoil from doing? Where is the edge of your courage? What would have you play your edge? What would expand it? And how would it be to give yourself permission to say 'none of these right now'?

Direct Action

Direct action is bodily intervention that aims to stop activities which harm: people (such as lying down in front of tanks), other-than-human beings (such as putting dinghies between hunting ships and whales), or the land (such as occupying ancient woodland threatened by development). River protectors at Standing Rock in 2016 hoped to defend all three. Harm is occasionally prevented, but more often the biggest impact is that the issue makes mainstream media, throwing a light on travesties of justice that might otherwise slip through in the fog of apparent normality. Because of direct action, most people now realise we should be very worried about fracking. Direct action made the public aware of secretive, middle-of-the-night deportations of frightened men, women and children who'd come to the UK to escape persecution. And direct action has opened hearts and minds to the painful fact that Earth's sixth mass extinction really is happening, and that we should all now be standing up on an unprecedented scale to insist, 'Not in my name.'

Taking part in direct action can appeal to the maverick in Trembling Warriors as a way of brandishing their flame, but it's good to think beyond the event. Before engaging in civil disobedience, you should reflect on whether you're willing to risk being arrested. As we've seen, idealists don't always anticipate consequences... so if you're considering civil disobedience, do some research first. My own experience of being taken away from Waterloo Bridge during the Rebel for Life action was surprisingly relaxed, but being approached by files of officers in high vis jackets isn't for everyone. (There are other things I fear more). Being held for sixteen hours at Walworth Police Station was a calm if uncomfortable experience: an opportunity for singing, movement, writing, meditation and resting. I found it impossible to sleep due to the bright lights and noisy air con, but food came in request, and the staff were kind and courteous without exception – even the ones who took my DNA, which rankled at a primal level. But from the many stories I've heard, it seems that police officers' attitude to activists varies enormously, depending on the offence, the overall strategy, the individual officer – and activists' attitude to *them*.

Even if you're willing to be arrested, it's worth finding out what offences you would be committing, and what the potential penalty – or sentence – could be. The 'Stansted Fifteen' chained themselves to a plane to prevent the deportation of frightened men, women and children who'd come to the UK to avoid persecution (some of whom have since been acknowledged as legal citizens). They were charged not for peaceful civil disobedience, but under laws designed to prevent acts of terrorism. Similar powers were used just weeks earlier to imprison three men who had climbed on to lorries at a fracking site. The fracktivists were set free on appeal, but if the corporation-backed right wing continues to gain strength in Europe and the States, appeals may be less successful in the future. Corporations are moving to weaponise injunctions, constricting freedom for peaceful direct action.

For Simon Blevins, one of the fracking protesters, being jailed for several weeks was 'shit but worth it'. Prisoners who lived locally knew about the site, and encouraged him and the others to carry on protesting when they were released. Although they had unpleasant experiences in jail, the three attracted the mixed blessing of mass media attention, as the first environmental activists to be imprisoned in the UK since 1932. Future activists could find themselves serving full terms, in more hostile environments. But many are willing to take the risk. As Extinction Rebellion co-founder Gail Bradbrook puts it: "When a government fails to protect the lives and livelihoods of its citizens — as in the case of climate change — the people have the right to rebel."

Extinction Rebellion (XR) was launched in October 2018, with three demands for government:

1. **Tell the truth**

Government must tell the truth by declaring a climate and ecological emergency, working with other institutions to communicate the urgency for change.

2. **Act Now**

Government must act now to halt biodiversity loss and reduce greenhouse gas emissions to net zero by 2025.

3. **Beyond Politics**

Government must create, and be led by, the decisions of a Citizens' Assembly on climate and ecological justice.

The direct action group swept into action just weeks later, closing several bridges in London. Eighty-two were arrested, which was their intention: to show the world that people are prepared to give up their liberty to defend Life against 'climate emergency'. Over the next few months an extraordinary self-organising took place, with an evolving structure, skilful communication, and meticulous planning - all underpinned by love and respect. Then came worldwide actions, with thousands of people willing to be arrested, forcing governments into (albeit slow) action on climate change. How XR evolves remains to be seen, but it has played a pivotal role in shifting the narrative around climate change.

All XR activists are invited to consider whether they are willing to be 'arrestable'. For some, a potential opportunity to have their say in court is a powerful incentive to civil disobedience, but it's good for sensitive idealists to pause and reflect on this; to come to a 'slow yes'. Whether or not you are allied to XR, consider carefully how you would manage any disruption to your life: do you have the support of your loved ones? How will your work be affected if you're convicted? Make sure you've thought about how you would cope in prison, and also consider what it might be like to go through the rest of your life having been in prison: how it might affect your family and relationships, as well as future employment, getting mortgages, and travelling abroad. *Then* follow your heart.

Be prepared too for the possibility of physical harm: whether in the action itself (dangling from bridges, stopping traffic, climbing trees, being chained to vehicles or glued to trains) or from heavy-handed treatment by police, security forces or ordinary people angry at being disrupted. However, effective direct action is usually peaceful, sometimes even silent – but always dramatic. Sometimes there are clashes between tough warriors prepared to disrupt society to get their message across, and those who don't want to inconvenience others – whether through genuine caring, or fear of reprisal., or both. There are many ways to be present at direct actions, supporting others but staying safe. High risk roles need only make up a small percentage of those present. Although not all events involve fights, arrests, or physical danger they're possible every time, and could have lasting traumatic effects on tender souls. Training in de-escalation and non-violent direct action (NVDA) can reduce the risks; yet you may still face tasers, tear gas, water cannons, and in some countries (perhaps soon in the UK), guns. Such violent weapons are said to be for controlling rioters, but are increasingly used to silence peaceful protest. Don't only expect direct action to be filmed: *plan* for it to be filmed. XR have trained legal observers who note down everything that happens during an arrest to ensure fair play, liaise with family members, and are invaluable companions on what would otherwise be a lonely trip to the waiting police van.

Some activists, of course, have no wish for their action to be filmed: not only is what they're doing illegal, but it's a form of terrorism. For example, several years ago animal rights activists were sending letter bombs, pushing faeces through letterboxes and digging up the corpses of farmers' relations. Needless to say, their action didn't achieve anything except hostility, and a lot of people were frightened and distressed. Such action usually emerges when Trembling Warriors are carrying psychological wounding they haven't addressed, and haven't learned to use their fire constructively. Even in legitimate action Trembling Warriors, in a passion of fury, can be provoked into to unleashing their hidden fire in retaliation to heavy-handedness or taunts. At a biological level, lashing out at your attacker is often a highly appropriate response. However, in a direct action situation, it only escalates conflict. If you get drawn into fighting, you're more likely to be hurt, but also you risk damaging the cause you're trying to promote. XR made one of its priorities offering NVDA training to all rebels across the country. None of this is to say there is never a time for fighting to protect what you love, and the need for warriors to go into battle may grow as economic, environmental and societal crises come to a head.

Aggressive behaviour also provides golden opportunities for arrest. If you are arrested during direct action – which can happen even if you've remained peaceful – the most powerful thing you can do is walk or be carried away with the police quietly, and with dignity. Gentle and sincere young activist Esme North was arrested in direct action at the Preston New Road fracking site. Shortly afterwards she wrote an article for *The Guardian*'s 'Comment is Free'.

> While governments, the police and the courts defend such corporations in their reckless pursuit of profit, we have no choice but to turn to direct action to stop new fossil fuel infrastructure. This is by no means the end. We still have our friends, our creativity and the determination to blockade a fracking industry that threatens our shared survival. History teaches us that non-violent civil disobedience has a powerful precedent in radically shifting the narrative and bringing about justice. So we will continue, until we win.'

When we met, Esme was awaiting sentencing and unable to say much about her experience. But in our conversation, she expressed a mature view of the Preston New Road action as part of a bigger, longer term movement to which she remains committed.

Launching into a direct action is like entering dangerous rapids. You've made your decision and done the planning some way upstream, but there can be no assurance you'll emerge safely. Your heart races with fear, but your strong conviction has you plunge in. Then, once things have begun, you're committed. With short rapids you're on the other side before you know it; others unfold more slowly, and require endurance. You have to ride the times of waiting with patience, and then navigate the buffeting twists and surges like a skilful diving bird: relaxed but aware, ready to adapt your tactics as you go.

If you are drawn to plunge into direct action, you will be far safer and more effective if you do it with a group, as part of a well-planned strategy. You'll need courage, collaborative and self-management skills, and if things turn bad, resilience and plenty of support: before, during and after events. If you don't think you possess these qualities, but still have an urge to act, your experience will provide a good opportunity to develop them.

Direct action is powerful and effective; thrilling and high-risk. And it brings an unforgettable sense of community and camaraderie. At one level it's good for raising the profile of an issue, and sending a message to the state or corporations that life-harming policy isn't acceptable. At another, more primal level, it's the adrenalin-charged rush alongside others into a high-stakes battle, to defend what you love. But remember: you don't have to take part in civil disobedience. It's just one way of acting for Life – the most extreme way. As XR's Larch Maxey points out, every contribution is of equal value, whatever role someone chooses to play: big or small, whether they've done it for years, or it's their first time taking action of any kind. "99.5% of the work is behind the scenes, supporting the action. If you're not prepared to risk being arrested, there's plenty more to do."

Any organisation trying to bring about change through direct action *needs* plenty of people who prefer to deploy their skills away from the frontline: organising events, running training sessions, updating websites and social media, talking to the press, or providing much needed emotional and practical support: all are necessary for success. And if, having considered, you don't want to get involved in direct action at all, that's perfectly alright. As we'll see, there are many other ways to be active in service of Life.

Protest

Polite requests such as petitions are useful for stating a case and raising awareness, but seldom lead to change - and never when wealth or power are being clung to by vested interests at the heart of government,. That well-guarded, secretive heart is what activists can only reach through mass protest movements, which emerge when it becomes clear that traditional politics won't succeed. Protests manifest in large numbers of people coming together at centres of power to say 'This is Not Alright' - whether about Brexit or climate change, war or mass extinction.

The will of the people is seldom respected by those in charge (in the Brexit sham, the 'will of the people' was of course manipulated into a fake and transparent shield for utterly cynical politics). The few who benefit from the status quo grip their interests protectively, and don't let go without a huge struggle. When people want policy that protects ordinary people or our precious biosphere, it frustratingly and regrettably has to be forced on governments; won through protest.

The chants, whistles and sirens, myriad faces, voracious media, and heavy law enforcement at a protest march are exciting for some, but a hedge-dwelling idealist's worst nightmare. You could of course choose stay at home, watching events unfold on Instagram and Twitter: you can lend energetic support and help shape public opinion on social media in ways that weren't possible until the last couple of decades. Passionate Remainer Jim told me he would never go on an anti-Brexit march: he'd be "afraid of it getting out of hand". His concern is partly for himself, and partly that any violence would be contradictory to the purpose of the march, and could damage the cause. But he also spoke of a fascination, a curiosity about what happens in the moment when anything tips over into violence. Perhaps we don't only tremble at the thought of the aggression we might meet: we tremble because we are afraid of our own fire.

Since 2016, though, a lot of reluctant activists have been on protests for the first time, as political and environmental stakes grow higher. And they often find something remarkable happens to them. They discover a sense of power, courage, agency and connectedness seldom experienced elsewhere. Like starlings in a murmuration, they're carried along by common purpose, the magical 'flow' that happens when individual psyches merge into the whole. Such a feeling can evoke courage people have seldom experienced before, and they grow in the process. Rosie, who lectures in Social Sciences, had never been on a protest.

> "Given my topic, I don't feel it's appropriate to be seen expressing political views. Plus, I worry about what people will think: I'm always anxious to make a good impression on others. But I did go along to the People's Vote march. Before the 2016 referendum, I saw people campaigning for Brexit and I thought they were mad: it was never going to happen, is what I thought. Then I was bowled over by the vote, and I felt bad that I hadn't campaigned for Remain - it felt like a dereliction of duty. I really never believed it would happen. So I went on the march. We were late arriving, and as we got there others were leaving - but that felt good, as if we were stepping up as they were stepping back. A helicopter was circling overhead all the time, and in that moment, I thought, 'Go ahead, take my face. I don't care.' It felt so important, as if the whole world wanted the same thing - though it didn't feel like that the next day, when nothing had changed."

Protest movements aren't only about a display of outrage: they involve a lot of strategic and tactical thinking. The Green Party's Natalie Bennett tells in an article for *Resurgence* magazine how two Sheffield women were arrested on private property for trying to stop tree fellers proceeding with their work.

> "A couple of days later, the (tree) protectors had an answer... someone was employed to paint a householder's gate under a tree contractors were due to cut down. Police were left scratching their heads: if the law was being deployed to protect workers' ability to proceed, which workers had priority?"

My own first experience of activism was a protest. In 1993, I joined a march protesting live calf exports. There were marchers young and old, someone in a wheelchair, a couple who looked (to me) like teachers, and others wearing combat fatigues. I was in my new fleece jacket: a multi-coloured splurge of pastels, which I hoped gave me a suitably 'alternative' look. The march set off: placards were waved for the television cameras, and I chatted with a nice middle-aged woman who was indeed a teacher. Presently we arrived outside the house of our MP. Someone began chanting, "Your head, on a plate!" Others gradually joined in, but I felt my body tighten: I didn't want anyone's head on a plate. Surely we were against cruelty and violence? One part of me was saying, 'I don't like this', and another said, 'I should join in: for the animals'. I pictured frightened calves crammed into hot lorries, eyes rolling in distress, and made myself join in the chant, although it died on my lips. Police cars arrived, which had an inflammatory effect: someone in combats shouted, "Let's shit in his garden!" I left with the teachers. Walking back, they told me about the 'rabble' who turn up at most protests. In my attempt to make sense of the day I cast the lads in combats as 'baddies'. I realise now that they were clearly angry, although probably not about animal welfare. They may have struggled to articulate what they were angry about, but their anger was real. How they chose to spend their day was the trouble they had gone to, to express their rage.

When I remember that day, two things stand out. My body was urging me to leave once it grew violent, but initially, my mind overrode it. I didn't agree with the aggressive approach, but I was also afraid of it. Some people are that kind of warrior, and perhaps we need them; I don't know. But I do know I'm not that kind of warrior. The other thing I remember: on Monday morning, a colleague said to me, "I saw you on television yesterday; I recognised your jacket."

Live exports still continue, and are still protested. It can be depressing when protests don't bring about immediate change; it can feel as though you and your team have 'lost'. But protests never achieve their aims on the actual day (that would be 'giving in'), being part of a longer term movement towards change. Massive demonstrations in 2003 didn't stop the invasion of Iraq, but did inform political action and help develop later movements: the Climate Camp was informed by the anti-war protests, and UK Uncut and Occupy grew out of their tactics.

George Monbiot, in *Out of the Wreckage*, dedicates a chapter to how protests could achieve much more practically. A natural strategist, he lays out step by step how marches could achieve far more by putting as much energy into an impactful format as organising coaches and painting banners. XR did just that in April 2019, with meticulous planning that covered all bases, but also allowed for spontaneity. Protests need strategists. Like direct action, they also require willingness to remain peaceful under provocation. Today, protest doesn't attract the violence it did just a few decades ago: disenfranchised young people have found a more peaceful, constructive voice. But crowds can be volatile and unpredictable. The higher the numbers, the more difficult it is to plan for and manage on the day (and the easier it is to 'get lost' in the crowd!)

Many protests have an 'alternative' flavour: whistles, drums, songs in praise of the Earth, hippie or carnival clothes, eloquent statements of love and fury. In other words, they're culturally maverick – and therefore less likely to speak engagingly to policy makers who have very different lifestyles and frames of reference. What would it look like, and how effective might it be, if everyone on a protest march wore a suit instead of combats or hippie layers (or multi-coloured pastel splurges)? Two XR activists did this when they glued themselves to the top of a DLR train at Canary Wharf, and the impact was shocking. What happens when protestors speak calmly in facts and figures, not just songs and chants? When we offer a list of measurable alternatives rather than demands for things 'now' and prophesies of doom? We are far more effective when we meet policy-makers and institutional leaders where they are: look like them, speak their language, show up as human beings they can relate to. The impact on traditionalist television viewers, shoppers, and social media users is very different, too, when they see people who look like them lying down for a die-in. We can't complain about those who can't hear our music, unless we are willing to hear theirs. Can radicals be inclusive enough to do conventional? XR needs to include

To join a protest, you'll first need to put in the effort to get yourself to wherever they're happening (the main ones are almost always in London or other major cities). For big marches you'll need to be able to endure a lot of noise and human bodies, and have a 360-degree tolerance for uncertainty, and willingness to be seen by the world protesting your cause. It also helps if you have the creativity to come up with a photogenic banner...

However, not all marches are fraught occasions. I joined Extinction Rebellion's Earth March for Life as it passed across Dartmoor, just north of my home, over three days. At times there were just three of us marching: Anna, with her eleven-month-old baby on her back, Sarah, who had walked the entire route from Land's End with a dodgy ankle, and me. It was a little lonely, carrying our banners through the mist. But it was also beautiful, and companionable. And we were supported by two fantastic elders, who cheered us along and kept us safe on winding lanes. Carrying the XR banner along the road from Tavistock to Exeter we, and all the others who joined the march, landed in the national consciousness as part of a much bigger story, as other marches made their way from Wales, and from the North, to converge at Westminster, as so many marches have done before. But do marches without direct action achieve anything?

Politics and Media lecturer David McQueen is a long-term activist who has lost count of the protests he's taken part in. In 2016 he accompanied his daughter Isobel on her first march, in support of the Campaign for Nuclear Disarmament. They heard some of the same speakers David had heard on similar marches, making similar speeches, more than thirty years ago.

> 'The peace rally on August 2nd 1914 in Trafalgar Square, on the eve of the first World War, failed to halt the calamity that engulfed Europe. The rally of over a million in Hyde Park in 2003 failed to halt the invasion of Iraq. Was this demonstration to join the list of protests that governments in Britain have ignored? Yet without protests we would not have the vote for working class men, women's suffrage, or a welfare state to protect the unemployed. From the Chartist rally of 1848 to anti-apartheid protests, poll tax protests, climate change protests and peace protests, Trafalgar Square has been a crucible for social and political change.'

When we march, we march not because we *expect* to make a difference, but because we *might just:* even if not today, then perhaps tomorrow.

Undercover

It's not only fear that causes warriors to tremble: those who go undercover are up close to the horrors of what they aim to expose - often even having to perpetrate those horrors themselves. Three activists went to work undercover for vegan charity Viva! at a 'Red Tractor' approved pig farm for three months. They filmed dead piglets alongside their mothers and siblings in narrow birthing crates, routine illegal tail docking, and piglets who were killed by being bashed against doorframes, with no checks to see if they were actually dead. Frightened pigs being loaded onto lorries bound for slaughterhouses were given electric shocks, and when they fell over, they were shocked into getting back up. Millions of pigs across the world are suffering like this right now. It's distressing enough writing about it; I wondered about the impact on tender activists who undertake the work. I contacted Juliet Gellatly, Viva!'s dedicated and energetic CEO, and she put me right immediately.

> "Somebody who's really sensitive wouldn't be chosen for undercover investigations; they wouldn't be the right person. You *have* to be able to do it without damaging yourself. That's really important. I've investigated and covertly filmed factory farming for twenty-five years. It's very challenging on many fronts, not least emotionally. I've also filmed slaughter, but I won't do that any more. I know my limits. Of course you get upset about what you see happening to animals, but if we didn't do it, all this would be happening behind closed doors and out of the public eye. You have to find mechanisms for coping. That's where it helps being part of a national organisation, so you can get your story out to the public. If you were doing it on your own, you'd see all that suffering, but then what would you do? If you couldn't find anyone to publish your investigation, you could be left holding

> on to a lot of negative emotions and feel helpless. But when your footage is used as part of a campaign you get feedback: people from all over the world telling you they've stopped eating meat after seeing Viva!'s exposés. To keep thinking of that is one of my coping mechanisms. Filming secretly at night is hard enough, but working undercover takes another level of resolve and strength. The people we employ have often gone undercover before, and not necessarily for animal welfare. Sometimes they're journalists. And they are able to follow it through, which is essential. If you challenged the suffering you were seeing at the time, you could blow the investigation wide open."

Lars worked for PETA in the United States. One of his undercover assignments, lasting seven months, was killing chickens in a slaughterhouse. "I was hanging them upside down in shackles on a conveyor belt, where their throats were slit – if they were lucky. If not, they went along the line and died in scalding water where their feathers were loosened. I did the math, and counted that I killed upward of a million chickens this way."

A former Marine, Lars always had a strong belief that he could do anything he set his mind to. However, he was also readily touched: "Oh yeah, I can cry over animal harm." So he desensitised himself before going in on undercover assignments by making himself watch multiple videos of animals being slaughtered. He was appalled, but his urge to address the issue constructively meant it had to be done. "I was sensitive on the inside, and loved animals, but I had a hard shell around me."

He coped with the chicken factory for months on end only because he was able to suppress his anger, guilt and frustration, although doing so had its cost: "It made me have a poor outlook on society, and the people who don't take a moment to realise their food consumption habits and the impact it has on the animals and the environment. It took a physical toll and a definite emotional toll on me which will be with me most likely forever."

He kept going by reminding himself that "It all takes time. I was only a small part of what PETA were doing, and part of a long process. Twenty years ago, when I first became vegan, I had to drive thirty miles to get soya milk. Now I can walk around the corner and get it. Even though it's impossible to say exactly what difference any individual makes, it all adds up."

Lars managed to work in slaughterhouses for three years, collecting video and audio evidence of abuse, and writing reports. Then one day he was driving away from the slaughterhouse and a truck was coming towards him, bringing animals in. "For a moment, I had this thought that I could drive headlong into that truck, and stop the madness." Doing so would certainly have attracted media attention, but that didn't enter Lars's head at the time. "I just had one thought: to stop the madness. But I knew it wouldn't do any good: the animals on that truck would have been hurt, as well as me and the truck driver. So I didn't do it, but that one thought told me it was time to get out, and let others carry on. Some people do it all their lives and I admire them, but I knew I couldn't."

Although Lars was able to suppress his emotions for as long as it took to get the job done, he still doesn't like visual reminders of the horror he experienced every day. "There's a film about animal farming called Peaceable Kingdom which I can just about watch to show it to friends, but when I'm on Facebook I scroll past films about animal cruelty, because I can – I don't have to watch them now. They just hurt me inside."

Lars says to reluctant activists: "If you think 'I could never do that', then you won't. If you care about animals but hold back, think about those animals and look yourself in the mirror. If you can say to yourself, 'I can do it', then you can. If you can't, then there are still many ways to be an activist. Write a cheque, volunteer, write emails, whatever works for you. But do something.'"

I asked Juliet, was she ever concerned about retaliation? "We don't get farms retaliating, at least not yet. And there's not much they can do, because we don't break criminal law. If individuals want to break the law they do it off their own bat, not in the capacity of their work for Viva! We're a strictly peace abiding organisation."

Going undercover is not for most Trembling Warriors, although some mavericks may be drawn to it. For effective undercover work you need courage, the ability to completely detach from what you're witnessing, emotional resilience, and skills for reporting effectively and accurately on what you've experienced. Above all, you need to be able to wear a convincing mask, in order to lead a double life - and sometimes you have to keep that mask on for a long time, which in any setting becomes stressful for most people. If you do decide to go undercover, you'll need to have your fire well under control so as not to blow your own cover. And it's crucial that you have somewhere safe to (regularly) take any trauma, guilt about not intervening, or other uncomfortable emotions that arise. If you're sure you can look after yourself adequately and avoid detection, you may be perfectly placed to bust open some sinister closed doors, shining light into darkness.

Campaign

The word 'campaign' is military in origin, reflecting the fact that effective campaigns take a lot of organising. They involve coordinated threads of action including protest marches, petitions, email-writing, press releases, and sometimes legal challenges, as in the case of Friends of the Earth's Heathrow Airport third runway campaign. Campaigns aim to tackle the root causes of social and environmental problems, bringing them to the attention of policy makers through an educated collective roar.

Extinction Rebellion (XR) is emerging as one of the biggest campaigns of our time. Mothiur Rahman describes its purpose in an article for Resurgence magazine.

> 'Extinction Rebellion's message, and the need driving it, is this: time has almost entirely run out to address the ecological crisis of runaway climate breakdown, mass extinctions of species, and the unravelling of planetary systems that support all life. It is a movement for civil disobedience born out of a recognition that existing political institutions, national and international, are incapable of generating the political will to meet the urgency of the time.'

XR uses a 'theory of change' based on civil disobedience as a tool for social change, and bringing governments to 'dilemma situations'. It has found that respect is a good predictor of success, and so it has encouraged respect: in communications within the movement as well as towards other citizens, the police, the media, and even governmental and corporate leaders. This successful strategy makes the movement immensely effective - and a spin-off is that local groups and project teams everywhere have come together to create loving communities, something Western society has been starved of for so long.

XR also has a carefully thought out strategy, involving a wide range of co-ordinated events conceived and supported by groups holding various threads, from political strategy to wellbeing to actions. For motivation, organising, wellbeing, collaboration, creativity and action, it's exemplary – companies can only dream of having employees as motivated, effective and team-spirited as XR. Like anything else it has its tensions and conflict, but is what it is because everyone is welcomed, shown real care and appreciation, and there because they care passionately about what XR's aim: to bring the urgency of climate change to the inescapable attention of policy makers and all of us, through direct action in which people are willing to be arrested.

> 'Being prepared to be arrested and face possible fines or prison is part of the Extinction Rebellion movement. Many of those demonstrating share a willingness to sacrifice personal freedom in order to bring media attention to the urgent risks of climate collapse happening within the lifetime of children now growing up.'

All campaigners want a high profile for the issue they're passionate about, but reluctant activists should be aware that publicity for a campaign can sometimes generate a backlash. Ann-Marie Cockburn has been campaigning for the legalisation and labelling of drugs since the death of Martha, her fifteen-year-old daughter who accidentally took an overdose. She told her story on Radio 4's Woman's Hour.

> "Martha's story was taken out of my hands and was online within 24 hours, and I just couldn't believe what I was reading and seeing. I saw the first interview the day after she died: I was being attacked online, and so was Martha. I couldn't believe what I was seeing, but that also empowered me to not care what anyone thought, because I know the truth of my child, and of the type of mother I was."

Ann-Marie wanted the truth to be known, and to make a difference, so she grew from 'an ordinary mum' into an effective campaign leader. With any kind of action, we all need to find our own best way of engaging in order to be effective: to grow clear about what works best for us, and what we find works best for others, and therefore what needs to happen in the space between.

Anna Lunk is a seasoned ethical campaigner. Clear-minded, knowledgeable and courteous, she helps on Green Party street stalls in the run-up to elections, is a parish councillor, and has been involved in many local campaigns.

> "I was born into an activist family, so it didn't seem strange to me: activism was just what people did. I grew up going on CND and anti-war marches in London in the sixties, and in my adolescence, I was out leafleting before elections. I'm full of admiration for activists who didn't grow up with it being the norm, who've done it from scratch." "I prefer it when we're asking people to do something specific, such as sign a petition about fracking. I don't like pushy people, so I don't like being a pushy person. If I'm handing out leaflets on the street and someone wants to walk past without making eye contact, they're probably in their thoughts, and I respect that. But if it was something I felt really strongly about I might break into their thoughts: for example, if there was talk of fracking in our village."

Engaging people on the street isn't for everyone, but Juliet Gellatly of Viva! says volunteers mostly find it can be surprisingly enjoyable.

> "We have lovely people who go out there on the streets and engage the public, telling them about our work. You might worry that engaging with the public about farm animals will be confrontational, but it's not – actually, far more people thank us than challenge us. Our job isn't to

> lecture or argue, it's to have positive smiley faces about the difference we're making. We get a very positive response from the public: there are fewer and fewer who challenge us because people are aware of the issues now. When I first started doing this more than twenty years ago, people didn't necessarily believe what we were telling them, and nothing was going to put them off their Sunday roast. But today, with social media, most of us have seen images of factory farming, and they know we're telling the truth. There's still work to be done though – for example, most people on the street wouldn't be aware that male calves are taken from their mothers within a day of being born, and are shot. But everyone these days knows someone who's vegan, or vegetarian. Most of us know there's something wrong with the way we farm animals, even if we don't know the detail."

To run an effective and prolonged campaign you need, first of all, a heartfelt passion for the cause. Campaigns require knowledge, commitment and organisation. But anyone can contribute to a campaign: they always need volunteers including fundraisers, people with IT skills, natural administrators, and people good at finance. Some idealists may find the 'back office' aspect of campaigns a bit admin-heavy. You could offer to give talks or run street stalls if you're inclined towards extraversion; if you're more of an introvert you could write blog posts, take pictures, run a social media page, or simply stuff envelopes. Just call or email the campaign for what you care about most, and find out what they need that you can do. And if there isn't a campaign for what you care about most, you could start one...

Campaigns aim to change policy. Another way to address that is, of course, in the realm of politics.

Politics

The world of mainstream politics is treacherous and unforgiving, and a strange mix of urgent and archaic. Politicians risk mental health problems more than ever. Although inciting hatred is illegal, the press gets away with publishing articles that stir up attack frenzies, and threats of violence and murder for some political figures are a regular occurrence. (And of course, those doing the attacking see themselves as Warriors, speaking truth to power. We can all hurt each other when we get caught up in narrow-minded ideology, and when we resort to spite instead of reason.) Behaviour until recently considered unacceptable has gradually become tolerated. And in an arcane, patriarchal system, women suffer most. Parliament, sadly, is perhaps more than ever no place for a sensitive idealist.

Paula stood as a parliamentary candidate in 2015. An ardent, knowledgeable biophile and forager on a spiritual journey, she embodies the Trembling Warrior 'peace and fury' paradox: warm, generous-spirited and conciliatory, yet open in her anger with, and condemnation of, stupidity and violence. She is regularly knocked off course by the harshness of today's society, but she's never deterred for long. "I've always been motivated by guilt. We live in a society today where we're not supposed to feel guilty, or responsible; but we have to start taking personal responsibility."

She's right that guilt has been labelled a 'negative emotion' – as climate psychologist Paul Hoggett puts it, 'as if all guilt was of the kind that persecuted us rather than also taking the form of a loving desire to make good.' Since 2015, Paula's continued to be active in her local party. "None of us want to be doing this. I'd rather just live peacefully, but I have to leave a better world for my children, and everyone's children. I could cry just talking about it. But if I don't turn up, who will? I was hoping others would get involved, and we'd be able to develop a community of like-minded people, and but it just hasn't happened. It's the same old few of us doing what we can. I'm still a treasurer, but I've stepped back from being more active. For now, I really need to look after myself."

Paula is familiar with her own pattern of ebb and flow, and has learnt to trust in its organic rhythm. "I will find my niche again, but I don't know what it'll be yet. I think I'd be willing to protest peacefully and risk getting arrested, but I just don't thrive when there's personal conflict. Politics is too cut and thrust: there's so much in-fighting about issues people feel strongly about. These things have to be discussed, but when it happens on social media, it just becomes toxic. And anyway, when you're trying to influence events on the world stage, the power is always in someone else's hands and you can end up feeling hopeless. I'm more inclined to do things at a community level, where you can make a real difference."

Parish councillor Anna always supports the Green Party at national election time, but has no wish to be involved at a national level. In 2018, she said, "I find party politics to be quite frustrating. Things move very slowly, and there's so much bureaucracy. The power is in the hands of corporate lobbyists and the media anyway; there's a danger in politics that you just get depressed. And for me, the Green Party doesn't shout loudly enough about the things that matter: like climate change, and a fundamentally new economic model." The Green Party is caught in a need to appeal to voters in order to have any influence at all. This broadened, and inevitably watered down, its seminal message. Maverick Green influencer Theo Simon posted on Facebook:

> 'It's our job to tell people that the planet is on fire, since we are the ones in the best position to notice. Instead it feels like we must tailor our Ps and Qs to what is electorally acceptable, not be alarmist, keep it sweet with the media etc..... I would like to see the Green Party become the party of climate emergency, because the old timetables are now irrelevant.'

In 2019 the Green Party has been quick to engage the rising mainstream awareness about climate change, and still has the sanest, most Life-protecting and Life-enhancing policies, by quite a long way. As people grasp the enormity of climate change, Green Party results in local elections reflect a growing mainstream concern. But it still needs either Proportional Representation to gain more than a handful of seats in Parliament– that, or the radical shift in public consciousness that may just be beginning.

In today's mainstream politics you need to be tough, confident, able to think quickly on your feet, strategic, assertive verging on aggressive, and have a good memory for facts and figures (all of which dreamers aren't usually known for). You may be drawn to help create a new way of governance that draws on much older ways: a politics of wisdom, compassion, responsibility, integrity, and accountability; in service of health and wellbeing for future generations of all living beings. But it takes immense courage to embody all of these in today's political arena, so as to begin that transition. I stood as a Parliamentary candidate in 2015, and although my campaign went well, I discovered that I am not, and could never be, a mainstream politician. I'm at my best around people who are trying to be kind to each other, and I'm as unskilled in strategy and outmanoeuvring as most politicians would be in therapeutic counselling. Whenever I've dipped a toe back in, I've known myself to be out of my comfort zone; in the midst of a different tribe.

However, I (and you) don't have to be in the public arena, or even attend meetings, to support what a political party is trying to achieve. As with any campaigning organisation, there's a lot of work to be done. The biggest parties receive corporate funding that acts as policy bribes. Smaller parties can pay for some roles, but rely heavily on volunteer work of all types. Again, get in touch and say what you're willing and able to offer – or if you're up for a stretch, ask what you can do. You can be politically active without even joining a party by engaging with your MP: attend surgery, write, email or tweet, but be vocal as to what you believe our country's leaders should be prioritising, and what values should be guiding their efforts. And, of course, there are always petitions...

If you have a strong affinity with the land, wildlife and human community where you live, you may feel drawn to the town, parish, borough or district council, where you can influence issues from protecting wild spaces, to creating a more democratic process, to ensuring the most vulnerable people are cared for. But don't expect any less conflict or stress than there is at national level. Strong traditionalist characters, determined and excellent at getting things done, tend to get involved in local politics. There is a lot of detail, a predictable format, and set protocol about who does what, and when. Creative types may find council and committee meetings an alien and even hostile environment - but here, too, new models are emerging. The Flatpack Democracy is an inspirational initiative begun in Frome, where every councillor is independent (not aligned to any party). The experiment has shown that with party competition out of the way, a whole new motivation of service comes into play, and process is far more peaceable and democratic. Councils across the country are becoming more progressive in their wake.

Of course, you don't have to be a councillor to have a voice about local issues: in many cases you can attend meetings, and you can always contact the clerk to raise something on your behalf. When I contacted my own Parish Council to express heartfelt and detailed concern about miles of lost hedgerow habitat in the parish, the topic was added to the agenda for the next meeting. I discovered others had been expressing concern about similar issues, and the Conservation Society met 'to discuss extending the Society's brief to include conservation and enhancement of the natural environment throughout the parish.' Conservation and enhancement are subjective terms: for some, scalped hedges are tidy, and improve the view. But the wild beings of the parish are now represented by human voices. I proposed that members of the Society meet with landowners to discuss the ecology of hedgerows, the green veins of the land, with the aim of restoring 'habitat' - in other words, the homes and sources of food for myriad creatures. Wild life can be rapidly decimated. But given the chance, it can rapidly return to its former abundance and beyond.

Some say politics is the only way to bring about change, but as long as the developed world is so entrenched in neoliberalism, it's a long, slow (and often removed) process. But today's politics looks as though it might crumble, even during the time that elapses between me writing these words, and you reading them. Trembling Warriors who want to put their energy into bringing about a new kind of governance might want to check out Rising Up!, the organisation from which Extinction Rebellion sprouted. Their white paper lays out a synthesis of elements and practices designed to bring about a constructive alternative to today's politics, and has an excellent reading and resource list at the end.

Mothiur Rahman, in his article for Resurgence, describes a citizens' politics in which we can both claim rights and honour responsibilities to the greater good.

> 'Civil rights are measures which facilitate "participation in the community, in the political community". Civil liberties or rights would therefore include the right of assembly and the right to freedom of expression. In other words, civil liberties are those which promote a sense of political engagement between self and other. Not in the sense of party political, but political engagement in the sense of granting the right to experience meaning beyond that of the self. This is in contradistinction to most streams of western thinking that isolate the individual and reduce his or her experience to a private individual and isolated "consumer". Behind the rather abstract term of "civil rights", therefore, is the capacity to fulfil a longing: to experience a widened realm of what it means to be human, reaching towards others in political association and together towards political community.'

We know politics in its current form is broken, but as MEP Molly Scott Cato points out, we must be careful what we replace it with: a breakdown of democracy creates opportunities for the far right. We need a new politics that draws on the best of the old, and strips out the rest. A new politics will be unafraid to use words like love, fear, and intuition. It will need to include visionaries and sages as well as those who are more action-oriented. Decisions affecting people, land and wild life will be made by those closest to the issues. It will not only allow, but encourage, time for reflection before answering questions.

People's Assemblies are an effective way of drawing on a community's wisdom: several people speak from their knowledge on a subject, and then the community divides into small discussion groups, from which emerge opinions, suggestions and actions, which all feed in to the decision-making process. Proportional Representation in the UK would be a game-changer, but Extinction Rebellion has demonstrated that radical change is not only needed, but possible. Their model of extremely precise organising and planning combined with emergent roles, and *genuine* creative responses, collaboration, inclusiveness and mutual support, has so far shown how Trembling Warriors could have a role at the heart of a new politics.

Meanwhile, if you want immediate practical change, the Transition movement offers a real, sane, and often enjoyable alternative to politics along the lines of civil rights. The Transition Network is clear in declaring itself apolitical, but at its best can achieve all that local politics should achieve: a healthy economy that respects all living beings in that community, including the land. A quick search will show whether there's a Transition community where you are. And if not, you could start one - once you tap into the Network, you'll find abundant support and inspiration. Gentle idealists don't usually want to lead organisations for societal change, political or otherwise, but they can provide the spark to begin one. Then they might prefer to contribute through vision-holding, or supporting inner transition, while others tend to the outer work of infrastructure and administration.

Social media

Social media *could* provide ways not only for activists to connect with each other, but to share news about the state of the planet and threats to the human soul with those who are just waking up to what's happening. It started off that way. But inevitably social media quickly became less social, and more corporate. It still offers possibilities, but must be used carefully.

If you show up on an establishment list as an activist, online or otherwise, your posts may be screened and/or filtered. Algorithms control not only what you see and don't see, but what is seen and not seen by those who follow you. If people stop responding to your posts, you may feel discouraged and stop posting, although the reasons are probably complex and impossible to assess. If you're a prolific Trembling Warrior who needs time out, and you don't share content for a while, your views will automatically start to drop. If you're suffering a dip in confidence already, that can lead to a downward spiral until you crash, suffering withdrawal symptoms from the online affirmation you'd been getting. Algorithms can raise you up to great heights. They can drop you on the ground hard, too. Social media activists who go viral can become stressed not only by constant intrusive engagement, but by trying to produce enough content to maintain a presence. If they let it slip, they're prone to their profile collapsing, and for those over-identified with their online identity, that can lead to suicidal thoughts.

If the global trend to the right continues, and the division between Life protectors and corporate interests widens, your digital footprint could one day be used against you in a more direct way. There are parallels across the world and throughout history, and no reason to think it won't happen again. Let's hope it doesn't come to that, but it's probably wise to make conscious choices now about how you could be categorized in a dystopian future.

Of course, not all online activism is high profile. A good many sensitive idealists put long hours into campaigns such as Hope not Hate, which targets companies advertising in racist tabloid papers, or Facebook group BBC Tell the Truth, keeping up the pressure for honest coverage of climate science, and many, many more. If you have physical or psychological mobility problems, you can be an effective full-time activator without leaving your house. Although such things are impossible to quantify, could achieve much more in a few hours online than you would standing in a crowd of thousands. There need be no guilt in activating in whatever way suits you best - but do be mindful that low physical activity and isolation can both cause a slide into depression.

Social media has made it possible for young people (and introverts) to have an influential voice at last, which has been wonderful. But a huge problem amongst young people is social anxiety disorder: in a digital world where so many of the factors that shape healthy human interaction are absent, the potential for shaming, exclusion, spite, narcissism and other toxic behaviours is high - but you're hooked by the paradigm you seek to challenge. We know social media is highly addictive, and it takes maturity, discipline and detachment (which not all Trembling Warriors have in spades) to use it as a tool without becoming unhealthily dependent on it.

At its best, social media has proven to be a huge enabler of social justice and environmental movements, largely due to the hashtag: a social organiser that emerged spontaneously and dynamically from content generated and updated by users. Originally intended as a way to organise data and information, it's now a prime tool for people all over the world to respond immediately to political, social and environmental issues as they arise. It's changed the game for traditional news outlets such as the BBC, who were looking a little foolish when they didn't cover news stories going viral on Twitter. Mainstream media no longer has all the control over what people know, and much less power in influencing their opinions.

Hashtags, like any other tool, can be used for good or ill. But as we've seen since 2016, they're a perfect vehicle for spreading #fakenews and manipulating populations with malicious intent. Cambridge Analytica and others have used social media to influence the outcomes of recent elections – many of which left everyone genuinely surprised. There's no way of ensuring social media of any kind is used to promote democracy and free speech rather than coercive groupthink; it's simply become another arena for the struggle between the power and money of those who seek to control for gain, and the skill, ingenuity and creativity of those who seek to defend true democracy. But one thing's for sure: even if revolutions aren't televised, they will certainly be hashtagged, tweeted, Instagrammed and shared on Facebook. And (for now at least), there's nothing anyone can do to stop it. So until someone creates a well-intentioned, user-friendly, not-for-profit platform whose primary intention is to connect people working to protect Life, we have to live with what we've got, and make use of it in a way that works for us.

Rosie got in touch when I asked for stories from Trembling Warriors. She said, "I'm quite an introvert, and I don't usually put things from my daily life on Facebook; I'm more of a lurker. But I did share quite a few posts about Brexit. A friend challenged me, saying it was inappropriate to post about political issues in a friendship group. I really took that to heart, and it made me adapt what I do." She hesitated as she thought about what she'd just said. "But that's my platform; I should be allowed to speak out. It's probably about getting the balance right. I do still tweet about Brexit, but I won't retweet anything that includes swearing, or is really cruel."

Trainee therapist Edwin spoke of his ambivalence about social media.

> 'I'm growing more passionate about social justice and more moved by the sufferings of others, such as the situation with immigrant children in the USA at the moment, yet I feel I do little about it. Moving towards activism and advocacy has come to feel like part of the purpose of my second half of life. Yet, I am conflict averse. I can have the mildest disagreement with somebody on a Facebook thread and spend all day

> worrying. Each subsequent comment fills me with dread and fear. All day I will be distracted by these threads, or rehearsing counter-arguments in my head, and I find it hard to do anything else. Where I've experimented with this a couple of times, I've felt it isn't worth the impact it has on me. Arguing on the internet is probably not very effective anyway, but I recognise it has a very disproportionate effect on me and I'm not sure why. However, not responding has its consequences too - yesterday I read a very unempathic comment defending Trump's child abduction policy that left me feeling sad and angry for hours, and by not replying I didn't discharge this.'

Paula, treasurer (and treasure) of her local Green Party, was very active on social media when I first knew her. She would express her views passionately, honestly and often furiously. Many have been hugely inspired by Paula's eloquence, but inevitably it's backfired too. She said, "A lot of what I do, I do on a wave of feeling. I could be too sharp on social media; that was getting me into conflict. The effect on me was despair that folk could shut out from engaging. I have learned it is not an effective way of communicating: we have to do that on common ground, and work from there. There is still a need not to hide facts, but I'm trying now to develop a more gentle voice. I've been doing an Active Hope course (from Joanna Macey's Work that Reconnects) and it's been helping me with that."

When you lose it on social or mainstream media, those who share your passion might support you, but those opposing you can use your fiery outburst of anger to discredit you with those in the middle: the ones you hope to persuade. Impassioned outbursts have their place and are sometimes necessary to jolt people out of complacency. But they have repercussions too.

Paula's still on Facebook, but she's been experimenting with her use of it. She stopped altogether for a while, but found it too useful to reject completely.

> "I have to have periods of not going on social media for a few days, otherwise I find I'm just absorbing everything: negative environmental and social global news, warnings from science of the dire need to address the way we live on our planet, daily evidence of biodiversity loss and severe weather events, and the suffering of peoples caught up in injustice: I was internalising it all.
>
> Facebook is a good place for connecting with other people who feel the same as you do, but it's not the solution. It can be addictive to get 'likes' and positive responses to something you've poured all your passion into: you feel like you're not alone. I believe we need that daily reinforcement. But then you get someone you don't even know coming on to your page and being aggressive. You lose that humanity. And you don't change anyone's mind; it really is an echo chamber."

Remain campaigner Adam advises spending time on neutral social media sites such as your town's home page, to stay in touch with differing perspectives. During my own period of Facebook activating, I regularly engaged others in conversation on sites such as Radio 4, the New Scientist, RSPB, and the National Trust. I didn't have a strategy; it arose naturally out of following the pages. I seldom experienced serious conflict: partly because I used posts as opportunities to develop skills in accuracy, clarity, positivity, courtesy, and open-mindedness, and partly because most of posters already shared some common interests and/or values. Working on this edge was more enjoyable than arguing with hard right-wingers: my input was more readily accepted, and more likely to contribute to positive change. I also learned. Feedback helped me to constantly evolve my knowledge and understanding, and get better at wording my views.

In the summer of 2018, needing inner spaciousness to support the writing of this book, I suspended my account. After a day or so of reaching for the habit, I found I didn't miss it: in fact, I was soon happier and more relaxed than I'd felt for a long time. I realised I'd forgotten what pre-Facebook life felt like. When I became involved with XR early in 2019, I opened a new account. I had intended to simply check in once or twice a day, but it was as though I'd stepped into a shallow but fast-moving river. I was seduced by its powerful, dangerous tug. I soon found myself spending much longer on Facebook than I'd intended, feeling dragged down by my newsfeed, and tangled up in algorithms. Yet I found myself still diving in several times a day: clicking the 'f' without even thinking – a powerful reminder that social media is truly addictive. I had to exponentially develop my mindfulness practice to use it lightly. Sad, but true.

When we enter any new group or community, we're busy figuring out the rules of social interaction so that we can participate. On social media this can be at best bewildering, and at worst damaging to friendships and self-worth. If there's one thing I wold convey from my social media wilderness time, it is this: *Find ways to harness social media, rather than have it harness you.* Introverted idealists might dip in just occasionally, and make good use of privacy settings. Some choose to only post, and never scroll; this unreciprocal approach can appear arrogant to those who regularly like your posts, so you might want to explain up front why you're doing it. And crucially, don't expect the dynamics of online interactions to be anything like those of embodied interactions. What happens to you there is not a true reflection of who you are, the impact your voice has, or how you are valued by your friends.

Although for a rising generation social media has been around forever, it's such a recent innovation that all users, activists and otherwise, are lab rats in a mind game we don't understand. There's already a lot of support around for social media burnout, and in future we'll need more people able to hold online activists, helping them stay grounded in nature, embodied community, and values that support wellbeing so they can safely enter the fast-moving, thrilling but toxic, sweet but dangerous realm of online activism.

Write

John Steinbeck wrote: 'I believe that there is one story in the world, and only one, that has frightened and inspired us. Humans are caught – in their lives, in their thoughts, in their hungers and ambitions, in their avarice and cruelty, and in their kindness and generosity too – in a net of good and evil. I think this is the only story we have and that it occurs on all levels of feeling and intelligence. Virtue and vice were warp and woof of our first consciousness, and they will be the fabric of our last, and this despite any changes we may impose on field and river and mountain, on economy and manners. There is no other story.'

Like Steinbeck, most introverted idealists write: we can't help it. It's how we best express our interpretation of good and evil; our vision for humanity. Tweets or Facebook posts, emails or old-fashioned letters, novels or short stories, poetry or screenplay, journalistic copy, articles or blogs; many reluctant activists find writing to be the form of action best suited to them. Paul, an IT expert in his thirties, fears that his strong socialist views would be at odds with his necessarily non-partisan employers. He's also a very private person, and sensitive. But he loves writing, he's good at it, and he has things he wants to say. So his activism takes place on anonymous, untraceable social media accounts, and blogs where he publishes powerful, socially aware short fiction. Writing gives us time to reflect on what we want to say; to research, and review, and reshape as we go, until what we've written feels true. And we can read comments, reviews and replies when we are ready.

Novelist Paul Kingsnorth, who formed the 'antidote to activism' Dark Mountain project, explains in his essay *The Great Work* that 'creative writing – writing that takes a stab at being 'art'– comes from a place of mystery. It is not a product of the rational mind, of the explicable, definable surface. The source of art lies deep down in the darkest parts of our psychic lake, while the rational mind forms a meniscus on top of the water. This is why writing which works only with argument, reason, and logic fails to penetrate anyone to the level at which they really operate. Arguments are all very well, but they change little in reality. Nobody ever argued themselves into loving someone. Nobody ever argued themselves out of their deepest desires, fears, hates, passions.'

The transrational is indeed a Trembling Warrior's muse, or source. However, those with rational minds would probably find something to disagree with here. Activist writing can, and indeed must, take many forms: there are all sorts of readers, both practical and poetic, and so all sorts of voices are needed to address them. People tend to think what works for them would obviously work for everyone else, if only they'd be smart enough to do it. The internet is full of writing advice: don't write unless you feel passionate, write something every day; let your words take flight, make your writing accessible; find your unique voice, meet readers where they are. It's all helpful advice if you've developed sufficient discernment to cherry pick: decide what's right for you, and tuck the rest away somewhere for reference.

Writing with an authentic voice is important to idealists, but it takes courage and self-belief to resist the pressure of critics, editors, publishers, style guides, and marketeers to conform to what the mainstream expects. This is just as true of non-fiction as fiction. Allowing your naked and most authentic voice to emerge is work - and that work starts with recognising and trusting your authentic voice. We all have ways of accessing that voice: for some, it's shutting out other voices; others go to the source of inspiration (wild places, or a muse), and for others it's the judicious use of freeing substances such as alcohol or caffeine.

The physical act of writing may take place at a desk, but (unless you have short journalistic deadlines to meet, or are engaged in an unfolding social media thread) the *ideaing* is far more likely to happen when you are engaged in some sensory experience such as a walk in the forest, or in conversation with a kindred soul. You then have to hang on to those scraps of ideas using key words or images, carrying them until you can put them down on the page or screen. So it's good to be prepared for the muse to descend, and take your phone (though that could distract), or a notebook or voice recorder – but don't whip it out too quickly, or you'll kill the flow and never know what else might have come.

One form of activating is to reclaim what has been banished from writing over the last few decades. We've been taught to write efficiently. Sentences must be short and colourless. Perhaps tolerable in business, word-theft has permeated fiction too, robbing it of richness and subtlety. Efficiency has rendered unfashionable the long sentences that slowly and carefully unfold a complex idea; it has stripped out language that imbues words on the page with soul qualities – language we can *feel.* Profound truths are dismissed as clichés, sending us scrabbling for original ways to express ourselves, until our innovative usage is so abstract, it's either laughable or incomprehensible. And nice words like 'nice' are ruled taboo.

I learned to strip out soulful words on a writing course thirty years ago. During my corporate career, I mastered short sentences. I doubt my writing will ever return to the unselfconscious expression of my teens, but the writers who leave me curious, gasping, eager, or furious are those whose visceral sensory images stalk untamed across their pages. Brevity, of course, has its uses, in the same way that cutting back wild scrub benefits some species. But tidiness shouldn't be the main objective: it should be just one manifestation of endlessly diverse and dynamic forms of expression.

My friend Glenn Edney, an Ocean ecologist, spoke of 'putting his head above the parapet' with his radical book *The Ocean is Alive.* In the early stages of writing he'd told me he was worried about how his peers might react to his transrational approach. He was less concerned about the emotional impact of exclusion than risking his professional status as a scientist, and the implications for his ability to carry out what he sees as vital work. Later he said, "I realised I could only write the book if I came at it from a place of total authenticity, and so that's what I did. By the time it was published, I'd worked through any concerns about how it might be received by others in my field. After all, I'd stated my belief that the Ocean is a living entity in the prologue: there was no going back from that." The support of like-minded others was essential in Glenn's process. He wasn't going out on a limb alone; communing with people on the same limb made a difference to how he felt – and how he was perceived. Some of the colleagues who'd haunted his thoughts in that early stage haven't even read the book (as far as he knows). Some bought it, but he doesn't know whether they've read beyond the first few pages. Some loved it, and have asked to collaborate with him. One commented, "I may not agree with all you say, but it is very well-written." I asked Glenn, how did reality compare with his imaginings about how the book would be received? "It was pretty much what I'd thought," he said. "The difference was, it didn't matter."

Sensitive idealists may love writing, but it can lead to suffering, too. First, there's the pain of researching the difficult subjects we seek to confront. Attempting to be confluent with society, we may risk overlooking the traumatic effects of research until we're already more damaged than we realised, unless we have somewhere to take and work through the nasty taste left by immersion in toxicity. And then Trembling Warriors prone to self-doubt can feel discouraged: by critical feedback, or the absence of any feedback at all, or reading some else's brilliant words and comparing their own work to theirs. You may feel immensely vulnerable when your work goes 'out there' – especially if your sense of pride was hard-pruned by humiliation when you were small, to prevent you becoming too pleased with yourself. Some dread most that their writing will be criticised, rubbished or rejected. Others would rather have their work read and criticised, than see it fall into that awful void of oblivion. Some dread both, and procrastinate endlessly about publishing. Others keep putting stuff out there, regardless of how it's received, their inner vision providing sufficient fuel for the crafting.

Of course, some visionaries' contributions are only recognised long after their death, when it can be seen from a distance; in context. And some are never recognised at all – or at least, only by a very few. This is in part because reluctant activists hate self-publicising, and so much of their important work remains unseen in today's super-competitive writing world. If that's true for you, undertake developing your resilience. Keep on exploring new avenues until you find the one that leads somewhere – and keep seeking feedback from people you trust.

If your blog goes viral, or your book is published, or a magazine buys your article, you're probably going to have to do some extraverting at some point. Today you can't just write. In a culture obsessed with soundbites and images, you'll have to do publicity on social media, go to events, speak in public or even on the radio or TV – all of which are anathema for hedge-dwelling activists, even though they may long for their work to be seen. If you have shared the precious stuff of your soul, and mourned because it has fallen into a void, there are two things worth remembering. One is that most people aren't wilfully ignoring or rejecting your work; they haven't even *seen* it. And, *the reach of your work, and even the response to it, doesn't equal the truth or significance of the vision you've expressed.*

There's a saying, originally from a play by Edward Bulwer-Lytton, that 'the pen is mightier than the sword.' Although I wouldn't fancy his chances in an actual duel, ideas that emerge through the pen (or keyboard) can bring about far more powerful and positive transformation to society than fighting ever can.

The Arts

Art has been used throughout history to portray both beauty and suffering. It can use literal representation showing things as they are, or it can convey meaning, or it can dream of how things could be. In times and places where it's been risky to speak out against the ruling powers, art has been used as a way of saying what cannot be said directly. Art provides an opportunity to influence without having to enter arenas of potential conflict such as direct action, protests or politics. Works of art shape as well as reflect culture, and as we'll see, can even influence policy.

In *It's Bigger than Hip Hop,* M. K. Asante writes that the art activist, or 'artivist', 'merges commitment to freedom and justice with the pen, the lens, the brush, the voice, the body, and the imagination'. Artivism, whether subversive photography or graffiti, painting or cartooning, satire or songs, is far from safe and comfortable. It simply brings different risks. A Trembling Warrior puts their creation out there and churns with anticipation as to how it will be received. Will it at least jolt people out of their current worldview? That is all some 'artivists' ask. We all appreciate validation, but may not have a strong need for public acclaim - unless perhaps to help us change the world more effectively.

Art that brings communities together in a culture that wants to divide us has an activating effect, and like Transition, is a healing aspect of the fight for Life rather than an aggressive one. Artivism can also be a cathartic use of fire, bringing healing to 'Borderlander' wounds and Earth trauma. The effect of your art largely depends on whether it takes a transformative form, or simply leads you to represent stark realities: too much immersion in that can corrode tender sensibilities. Courtney Mattison addresses her anxiety about climate change by creating beautiful sculptures of coral reefs. Her idea is that the public might see a ceramic representation of a brain coral and think: "How gorgeous – I don't want it to die!" "I do privately vent and complain and tear my hair out," she told climate journalist Eve Andrews. "But then I get it together, and think about what will be productive in terms of inspiring change." The thing about art is we don't usually get to choose what emerges – as poet and embodiment therapist Sophia knows.

> "I find writing poetry very intimately connected to embodiment. My bodily experience and the images that emerge from them often form the base of my writing. I need to step out of the way and surrender to the energy that moves through me; it is a kind of channelling. It is often very passionate and revealing so sharing it can make me feel immensely exposed and vulnerable. It helps when I treat the poems as separate entities that want to come alive, want to be spoken, be heard. They have chosen to come through me so I owe it to them to share them with others. At times when I don't plan which poem to share (or to share at all) being tuned into my body and into the present moment (and through that what is happening around me) is what guides me."

In his essay for *Emergence* Paul Kingsnorth writes eloquently about the trust involved in the true creative act.

> 'In times like these, we are all in the process of transformation, and so is the world around us. The Great Work, the *magnum opus*, is the work we are all engaged in, whether we know it or not. The Great Work is the reassembling of the tiny shards of light into which the universe was shattered at the Creation. Every story we tell, every poem we write, if it is true, reassembles a tiny piece of this light, brings us back closer to the heart of the mystery. How do we know this? We don't. At the heart of art is the same paradox as lies at the heart of religion: we don't know

> anything. We can only act from our unknowing, with faith and determination.'

Most people are already tired of hearing facts about climate change, and seeing the numbers of species becoming extinct. It's important that these facts continue to be available - not only for people who appreciate data, but for anyone coming to the facts for the first time, as people will continue to do for some while. But once the facts have worn off, something else is needed. Art evokes emotion, and emotion engenders action. Cultural historian Julian Spalding said in a radio interview: "There's lots of art celebrating the beauty of the natural world, but not much new about the relationship between humanity and the planet. Not many artists are getting to grips with this; it's difficult to make an artistic statement about what is really happening, the fear and impotence about the state the world is in. But if you celebrate but don't warn, you're only doing part of the job." There are three types of artivism: one which engages people by showing what's happening, another which is more about creative responses, and another - the visionary - which shows *what could be.* If you are an artivist, you probably don't need to choose: if you simply make your art and notice what emerges, you will know what has chosen you.

Art not Oil are a young group who risk the wrath of powerful fossil fuel giants by creating installations to draw attention to BP and Shell's sponsorship of the UK's best known galleries and theatres. They use visual art, song, theatre and movement (see them on YouTube) to connect with audiences about fossil fuels in a way traditional protest can't manage. Several museums and galleries have already dropped their relationships with oil and gas companies as a result. Meanwhile, the Cape Farewell art project has sent over three hundred artists including photographers, dramatists, and sculptors and painters to the Arctic, where they have been inspired to create something in response. Most didn't want to be seen as activists creating 'propaganda'; the work they made after experiencing the Arctic alongside scientists has its own power. On the other hand, the BBC is always telling us that people want to hear bad news: and in their Wildlife Photographer of the Year competition, there are now as many images showing the devastation of Life as there are celebrating it.

Art that engages at a rational, informing level and that which simply arises through the artist's being moved, are both needed in the fight for Life: the more diverse ways we have of touching soul, the more diverse souls will be touched. That's the work of an artivist. Amitav Ghosh, in his book *The Great Derangement*, suggests that artists and writers are as responsible as governments for how our species' relationship with the rest of the biosphere plays out in the future: 'the imagining of possibilities is not, after all, the job of politicians and bureaucrats.' Imagining of possibilities is crucial if we're to dream into being a healthy, mutually enhancing future for people and planet.

Photographer Nick Danziger has been to Armenia several times to photograph isolated elderly people, raising awareness about a Red Cross project trying to help elderly men and women living in poverty in garages, surviving on scraps, and burning their clothes to keep warm. As Nick described in a documentary, it's stressful work - and not just because of the many technical challenges. While Nick was photographing an elderly amputee who'd been trapped in his room for three years, his translator was in tears. Later, Nick asked a government official whether his pictures make a difference to people's lives. She responded with symbolism: "If this is done constantly or permanently, it will become a sort of a monitoring tool. If our initiatives are working well, then the light will increase in the photos as well. If not, it will stay the same or decrease: that is, it will show that things are not working, and we should take additional steps."

Monitoring is an important aspect of activism. Just as geology monitors global patterns to predict earthquakes, and climatology monitors global weather patterns to predict storms, global activism must monitor global trends for emerging new forms of dystopia. In Cuba, artists have been arrested for protesting Decree 349, a new piece of legislation allowing government officials to shut down concerts, performances, galleries, and to halt sales of art and books if they don't comply with the strict list of prohibited subject matter. It also restricts artists from selling their work without government approval. This is how the mainstream has always tried to shut down the alternative, and we will likely see more of it in the coming years; so artists should keep an eye on what's happening around the world, and watch the way such a chill wind is blowing. As Martin Luther King said, 'Injustice anywhere is a threat to justice everywhere.'

Meanwhile, long-term activist Anna sees joy and locality as fundamental. "I've been involved in a project called Visible Ink, which put on evenings of themed music and poetry to raise funds for local causes: environmental charities, asylum seekers and refugees, and Amnesty. It's an all-round win: I enjoy performing; it raises money for worthwhile causes, raises awareness of the issues and, hopefully, gives the public an enjoyable evening." Artivism will appeal to many reluctant activists as a powerful way of combining activism, creativity and pleasure whilst challenging, enriching, or shocking the cultural narrative.

Culture Jamming

Culture jamming aims to disrupt the worldview of those playing what I call in *The Game* the 'Sleepwalker' avatar, shocking us out of the hypnotic media and marketing messages that keep us entranced. Culture jamming can take many forms: for example, spoof stickers on the London Underground that look official, such as one asking commuters 'Travelling on the DLR line soon?' which on closer inspection protested an upcoming Arms Fair. Also in London, the Special Patrol Group hack urban advertising spaces with spoofs: one called out Volkswagen for its cynical attempts to make good after the emissions scandal. Adbusters are 'an international collective of artists, designers, poets, punks, writers, directors, musicians, philosophers, drop outs, and wild hearts' who create 'subvertisements' such as the MacDonald's disruptor ad 'Eat Fast, Die Young'. Grassroots culture jammers disrupt places and events with a flash mob, which Wikipedia amusingly describes as 'a group of people who assemble suddenly in a public place, perform an unusual and seemingly pointless act for a brief time, then quickly disperse.' Then there are the spontaneous individual acts of subversion such as #plaidshirtguy, who found himself standing right behind Donald Trump during a televised speech, and responded with exaggeratedly incredulous expressions before being removed.

These maverick activists hope such 'happenings' will evoke strong emotions that lead to behavioural change or political action. You can see the slack jaws, when people walk past a happening such as the 'die-ins' and other culture-jams staged by Extinction Rebellion (check out Blood of our Children on YouTube). By-passers' eyes are drawn, and their attention fully hooked, by the perceptual dislocation they're experiencing, their psyche trying to make sense of it, while their bodies go along on autopilot. Their worldview has shifted - at least temporarily: the soil has been fertilised in which future seeds will land.

In the US, the Yes Men demonstrate how 'lies can expose truth', creating and maintaining fake websites replicating those of their targets, which have led to numerous interviews, conferences, and TV talk show invitations. They've made use of these cunningly won platforms to make public announcements about corporate inhumanity, such as Dow Chemical's evasion of reparation for the Bhopal gas tragedy, an industrial accident that harmed and killed thousands of humans and other beings when toxic gases leaked from an insecticide plant. Watch the Yes Men's films if you have a free evening and a bowl of popcorn: they're good drama and hilarious, as well as being illuminating, thought-provoking and deadly serious.

Other disruptions to Sleepwalking culture include initiatives like 'Buy Nothing Day', an antidote to Black Friday, and 'True Cost', which invites people to compare the human and environmental cost of products to the sales figures. Anyone sharing their memes is taking part in culture jamming. Some Trembling Warriors do it reluctantly, worried that they'll hurt or offend someone who loves buying gifts, or making their home beautiful. We know we can seem like killjoys when we remind people that most forms of mainstream consuming are killing the biosphere. The lover in us is conflicted, but the ethical and visionary parts of us inevitably bring our focus back to defending Life. We have beautiful alternatives to consumerism to offer.

Culture jamming is a wonderful way to activate for the trickster maverick in Trembling Warriors, and also appeals to the hedge-dweller. Introverts find it an exciting way to be active but anonymous – in fact, check out Anonymous: the culture-jamming group of internet 'hacktivists' who take on corporations with their unrelenting moral stance on cyber-surveillance.

Some acts of disruption arise from anger rather than artistic or ethical intent; sometimes, of course, Trembling Warriors are motivated by all three. At times there's a fine line between 'brandalism' (culture jammers love their portmanteau words) and vandalism. Some culture jamming might do more harm than good, but in this stealthy and fast-moving form of activism, outcomes are impossible to predict or assess, and everyone has to make their best call.

Another powerful way of protesting the system is to opt out of it: to stop colluding, and withdraw consent. You can of course do so quietly, as does my eighty-eight-year-old mother, who refuses to shop in supermarkets so as to support her local economy. Opting out of any harming mainstream practice is Trembling Warriorship when it becomes uncomfortable. The young women (and men) behind Birthstrike may long to have children, but publicly choose not to procreate as a statement about climate change and societal breakdown. They have received abuse and rape threats for their stance. But we risk disrupting harmony even when, for example, we maintain a wildlife-friendly garden in a street that's a tidy, severe battleground against nature; or when we opt out of the family Christmas spending frenzy.

Trembling Warriors who aren't particularly maverick may fear the social exclusion that can come with opting out of the mainstream. Social exclusion can happen when we refuse to subjugate our true beliefs and preferences to fashion: for example, choosing not to wear labels, or buy the latest home décor, kitchen equipment or pet paraphernalia, spend money on a certain image to appear 'professional', own a smart phone, or be on social media. This can be a particular challenge for young idealists who (unless they have a strong maverick streak) are naturally, biologically even, seeking to fit in with their peer groups. That's why it's vital to find (or build) networks aligned with our values: people also doing their best to discern between what they believe is right, and the subconscious driver of 'I'd better, because everyone else is'. Some activists can become very conflicted around opting out: it's an act of courage to do what is ethical instead of what is seen as 'normal'.

There are risks to security (depending how you view security) when you choose to opt out of carbon emissions by living off grid; but there's plenty of support, for example the Alternative Living Group (perhaps ironically) on Facebook. Another possible risk is opting out of the mainstream workplace and committing your talents to something Life-enhancing, depriving the paid-slavery-and-destruction model of its units of labour (you). NHS therapists controlled by targets and outcomes speak of having to go by stealth to be kind to people. Some spend longer with clients than they're supposed to, by completing paperwork faster than the allocated time. "If they play time and motion with us, then we must simply play it too." Some have opted out by going freelance and offering lower rates to those who can't pay the full fee. They speak of experiencing an immense sense of liberation, as well as the satisfaction of contributing to a more equal society.

In industry, clothing company Patagonia opted out of Donald Trump's corporate tax cuts by donating all the extra profit to charities. It was a brilliant act of subversion, helping many good causes and making a statement, sparking thoughts and conversations about taxes.

Opting out is possible for not only adults in the system. Soon after I began writing this book, Greta Thunberg started opting out of school every Friday, to sit outside the Swedish parliament until they agreed to take significant action in carbon emissions. Her viral speech at Poland's Climate Change conference inspired students worldwide to join her in opting out of school on #fridaysforfuture, leading to arrests in the UK - and massively raised awareness of climate change. What could you opt out of, announcing your reasons for doing so, to challenge the dominant paradigm?

Sometimes opting out isn't a choice; it feels like the only possible thing to do. Hamish is a Maori, and a member of Ngatiwai and Te Waiariki peoples from Northland in Aotearoa/New Zealand. Like many of his generation, he never had the opportunity to learn the Maori language. For thirty years he'd worked as a commercial fisherman, but had a slowly growing awareness of the destruction that he was involved in. One calm day, while skippering a tuna boat, he leaned over the side and saw all around the boat, floating on the still surface, hundreds of tiny pieces of plastic. In that moment he knew he could no longer be complicit in humanity's thoughtless assault on the Ocean. He stepped out of his work, with no idea what he would do next. He attended community meetings with the intention of asking what could be done locally to restore the Ocean's health, but lurked at the back, too embarrassed to say anything because he couldn't speak the Maori language. His love of the Ocean was so important to him that eventually he found the courage to speak out. However, he found his community's relationship with the Ocean to be primarily an exploitative one, focused on financial gain, with no real sense of the bigger picture. Hamish now keeps bees, and sells delicious honey. He has returned to his family land, engaging with it in a way he'd never been able to as a child. He and his partner Ali are now working with my good friends Glenn and Janey, leading a Trust to support local people in monitoring and protecting their own patch of Ocean. Hamish had the courage to opt out twice: first from commercial fishing, and then from a community that wasn't aligned with his values. Doing so created the space for something new, authentic and exciting, with like-hearted others. He asked me to share this *whakatauki* (Maori proverb), which he described as "Ngatiwai and Te Waiariki traditional knowledge that has been somewhat ignored for financial gain."

'*E tangi ana nga reanga o uta, e mahara ana nga reanga a taima ta aha ra e whakamahana taku ora kia tina*' – 'When the land, river and sea creatures are in distress then I have nothing to be proud of.'

Indeed: in an economic system that causes such distress, profit is no mark of success. However, we don't all have to opt out of the mainstream workplace to bring about positive change, as we'll see in the next chapter.

Work

In *Hearing our Calling* I wrote about how the workplace has gone into overdrive in its zeal for bureaucracy above creativity, and profit before people and planet. Despite the masquerade of corporate responsibility, most players in the capitalist economy contribute, through their work, to destruction. The size of large companies means inevitable disconnects: no-one need feel directly responsible for harming unfamiliar species, or far-away peoples. The disconnect across departments, and between hierarchical levels, leads to stressed and unhappy workers - who could be doing something of value in the world. More of our colleagues than we might imagine suffer in such environments, where their authentic, altruistic self is compressed; stays hidden. Social workers, as well as NHS staff, speak of having to go 'under the radar' to demonstrate kindness: in a target-driven environment where efficiency trumps humanity, acts of care are often seen as acts of subversion. Some choose to leave, unable to enact the care they'd gone into their jobs for. "I have no job," said one, "but I still have my humanity." Perhaps more concerning are those who adapt and dissociate in order to conform - to be seen as 'professional'.

'Behaving professionally' used to mean behaving responsibly: taking responsibility for quality of work, and respectful relationships, and responding skilfully to situations: whether through strategy, or in the moment. But today, to be 'professional' means to cut ourselves off from our bodies, our emotions, and even our conscience to operate as servants or masters in a rapacious, competitive and exacting workplace. This can cause great stress for sensitive idealists, who typically find they have to hide their true gifts, and pretend they are what they are not in order to survive.

Everyone *can* potentially access the socially conscious part of themselves, but it's at the core of sensitive idealists, who are absent amongst directors of most large organisations. Had there been more visionary idealists occupying senior positions in industry in the 1940s they might have intuited, and raised, that creating synthetic chemicals and producing them *en masse*, would eventually poison our food, air, and water. When conscience is externalised (projected on to activists) it is seen as *other*, and therefore easier to oppose, or simply ignore. Industry may not welcome idealists, but anyone who performs the tough role of organisational conscience on behalf of the biosphere deserves our gratitude.

In 2016, new client Sue said at the beginning of her first session, "I don't know how you'll feel about having me as a client, given who I work for" (a global manufacturer of a 'food' indubitably harmful to health). I knew a little about her, and told her I was delighted: she shared my love of Life and was an extravert, and a feisty one at that. Sue wanted to develop an effective warrior voice. In her role she was well-placed to name 'Emperor's new clothes' policies masquerading as 'sustainable', and seed more soulful communication and decision-making; working toward a business model that genuinely respects people and planet, and enacts that respect rather than just spouting words about it. Every day, she does as Aldo Leopold suggests in *A Sand County Almanac*: 'Cease being intimidated by the argument that a right action is impossible because it does not yield maximum profits, or that a wrong action is to be condoned because it pays.' She draws on her courage to use soul language, wild words, at work: to keep a flame alive in the corporate environment.

Corporate giants exist as an integral aspect of our economy and society, and it looks as though they're going to be here for a while yet. If all biophiles shunned them and worked for ethical organisations, or became self-employed, then who would provide the moral compass for such organisations? Trembling Warriors like Sue, prepared to work on the frontline, actively influence the narrative. They also bring what they learn back into 'alternative' communities, weaving a much-needed bridge. The role of visionary outsider, as we have seen, is by no mean a new one. It's engaged in an ancient struggle, which in recent decades has taken up residence in the arena of the workplace.

If you're a Trembling Warrior wanting to be effective in the mainstream – that is, the public or private sector and most large charities – you need resilience: not only to handle the stress, fear and shame so present in mainstream workplaces, but also so you can keep your principles in clear sight, and speak out to challenge harmful practices. It's also crucial to have an encouraging support network, whether at work or outside: so that you're not left holding everything, and to ensure your soul stays nourished; 'topped up'. When we allow ourselves to bring our inner lover to work, that work can become both joyful service and play. We are activating when we allow the lover in at work: let him or her flourish expressively in us, and in our colleagues too.

Twenty-eight-year-old Harry, a teacher at an alternative school in the Midlands, recognised that 'the power had got out of balance'. Staff, parents and pupils had all previously contributed to the running of the school, shaping its playful, joyous, collaborative culture. However, the school secretary had amassed 'immense power' (we might wonder what she was afraid of.) Along with her assistant, she had gradually taken over the decision-making, introducing strict rules where there had been consensus. It may have been difficult and uncomfortable to work through a disagreement before, but everyone had learned from the process when it was held well.

Harry felt frustrated and furious that the progressive, hard-won culture of the school was being eroded. He used to fantasise about what he would say to the administrator, but couldn't summon the courage to do so. Her power was such that he felt paralysed; unable to challenge; the one time he'd tried it, she'd dismissed him as 'sulky', and begun manoeuvres to make things difficult for him with senior staff. He knew that the parents and most of his colleagues were 'on his side', but none of them dared to speak out, either – even to each other. Harry decided to leave at the end of the school year, but he wanted to leave a legacy: a gift to the pupils he'd come to love. So he organised an end-of-term meeting for staff, parents and trustees to discuss best practice. The administrator vetoed the meeting. The next time I saw Harry, he told me he'd since learned that in surfacing the issue, he'd provided a catalyst for open and constructive conversations between parents. I asked him whether he regretted challenging the administrator. "No way. It was time for me to leave, and it's opened up some exciting possibilities I wouldn't have thought about before."

One of the benefits of growing older is that a Trembling Warrior's fear sometimes subsides. Lecturer Rosie: "One thing that's made a difference is turning fifty. I'm now much less sensitive to what people think about me: if you like me you like me; if you don't, you can jog on. It's been hugely liberating. I recently raised something with my manager's manager that I thought was unethical. I'd never have done that before. And it was actually fine: he hadn't known what was going on and he welcomed the information. Things there are changing now, so maybe I did make a difference."

There are broadly three ways of activating through your work:

- Dedicate your work, paid and/or unpaid, to directly defending or enhancing Life: whether with an NGO, Social Enterprise, ethical company – or become self-employed, doing what you love best.

- Work indirectly for Life like Simon, a day trader who siphons money from the mainstream and feeds it into ethical initiatives, or Jack, who advises billionaire philanthropists on what to do with their wealth.

- Activate away within the mainstream workplace like Sue – though you need plenty of resilience and/or support for this one, if you're a sensitive idealist.

Teach

In discussions about such vital topics as food, the economy, land use, building, health, or renewable energy, at some point someone usually says urgently, "It all comes back to education." And so it does. There's an important struggle taking place for students' hearts and minds. Neoliberalism uses media, advertising, and the education system to shape people's view of reality and thus their behaviours, whilst biophiles use education to defend and nurture a balanced, holistic approach to Life.

Teaching can be a form of activating wherever you do it: at a school or university, in a company training room, on a workshop or residential course. You have a good platform to do some cultural myth-busting, and cut through the neoliberal norms. But even regardless of content, teaching is activism when you bypass the mainstream curriculum: opt out of damaging testing, give your students permission to take part in climate strikes, or subvert a process you consider detrimental to healthy education. One form of activism in the classroom might even be to encourage children to cook, or grow vegetables, or make music, where such essential development activities aren't included in the timetable.

Teaching is a position both privileged and vulnerable. People enter the space with ears and minds open, and maybe hearts and souls too. In a time-honoured transaction, one with knowledge, experience, and mastery in a certain field helps others to grow in that field. Yet when you step into the role of teacher, others instantly begin assessing: is this a valid transaction? Should I open or close to the person standing in front of me as teacher? The teacher-student relationship, like so much else, has been skewed by monetisation: consumers of education feel entitled to their money's worth.

An additional challenge is the disappearance of respect. A generation or two has grown up in a culture that negates authority: where parents consult children, world leaders have been morally discredited, mature community elders have all but vanished along with community, and preachers are a thing of the past. There has been a natural and necessary pendulum swing away from patriarchal over-control. But the resulting vacuum leaves young people floundering, trying to find their own way: sometimes doing it extremely well, sometimes not, and often missing (without knowing it) an important ingredient: respectful relationship to elders. All creatures must learn from their elders: jackdaws can only learn how to be a jackdaw by watching senior members of the flock.

Often, of course, many students engage in activism: steeped in learning, and with their flame burning brightly, young activists bring great energy and dedication to shaping the future they face. For example, medical students Ally Jaffee and Iain Broadley were frustrated by the virtual absence of food, nutrition and lifestyle in six years of training. So they took it on themselves to form 'information and innovation hub' Nutritank, for students and doctors rejecting the primarily pharmaceutical model in favour of addressing basic preventative health issues. Self-directed learning is certainly a big part of the future. But teachers contribute a precious ingredient: themselves.

Idealists make wonderful teachers when they know their topic well: bringing insight, integrity, rapport, authenticity, adaptability, inspiration and encouragement. But if they falter in a moment of self-doubt, students pick up on it – and can become critical and hard to please. Jean is an intelligent, dynamic woman who embodies all of the above qualities, and instantly recognised the notion of Trembling Warrior from her classroom experiences.

> "As a lecturer in complexity theory, I am invited to run modules on Masters courses at various institutions. I see this work very much as a form of activism. Traditional perspectives of what is professional and scientific assume the social and natural world works like a predictable machine. They have led to policies and strategies which have made the world worse, in my opinion. They contribute to 'one size fits all' management processes, and a search for the 'right'

method to achieve the intended outcome. And that's before we get into the impact of capitalism on climate change and social justice. Complexity theory is much more attuned to the nature of the social and natural world, pointing us towards systemic, contexted, dynamic, sometimes paradoxical approaches to change.

I'm passionate about the content I teach. And I'm passionate about the importance of *how* I teach: we, in the room, are a complex system. Can the medium of my teaching be congruent with the message of complexity? So I ask what creates our patterns of behaviour in the classroom, what makes *us* change..." which can turn sessions into a sort of reflective group therapy, and certainly draws on practices from Gestalt and Zen. It can also unleash any frustration with the wider course or the institution, and if I'm not careful, I open myself up to be a scapegoat. I am both facilitator of the process, and within the process.

The message of complexity requires from us high levels of authenticity and integrity. If our behaviours are the ingredients we put into the complex system, then together we co-create the future. Ergo, I have a responsibility to put into the system the best ingredients I can. To me this means I should be transparent; should not protect myself behind the screen of authority, should allow myself to be affected by the experience (and allow that to show), as well as 'creating an experience' for the students.

At the same time, I'm designing a process that balances conceptual learning with experiential learning and practical application, and being prepared to modify that design as things unfold. And being authentic without being needy, flexible whilst holding boundaries. Alongside all this process awareness, I'm sometimes conveying ideas from the history of science and philosophy, and sometimes summarising important ideas in science. Yet another part of my being monitors whether it's time for a tea break, or someone is looking lost. I feel under pressure to be amusing, charismatic, calm and guru-like, so I can draw them in with my charm, wit and insights, rather than set out on a path which requires hard work for us all.

This is all hugely challenging, and no wonder I tremble. I am constantly on an edge. Of course, to a large extent, it is a task I have set myself. There are not always support mechanisms in the wider institution that even recognise what I am trying to do, never mind offer support. If I'm there just for a short time, am I worth investing in? Do the permanent staff get involved with me and work through difficulties, or do they distance themselves if things get tricky? Do they see me as a person – or as a passing talking head, with the jury out on whether I'm good enough?

I find myself carrying more anxiety than normal, feeling unsure of what isn't being expressed, what is *really* going on, in the room and out of it. I don't always feel safe. And, whilst feeling less poised and more vulnerable than I'd like, I'm still aiming to teach holistically as well as teach holism. I'm moving between paying attention to individual responses, and exploring global geo-political issues. I'm trying to respond in the moment, and keep on track with a syllabus. And I'm trying to balance what students feel they want with (maybe I should not say this) what I think they need. Does their immediate response matter most (in line with the consumerist model of education), or how they come to see things in a few months, or even longer?

How can I be me in all this, with my intellectual and emotional limitations? How can I look after myself and find support? Should I be so anxious and (sometimes) ungrounded or is it just of my own making? How can I explore and surface some of the shadows and dynamics

> of the wider system in which the teaching is taking place and stay relaxed and confident? Indeed, I sometimes wonder, am I really good enough, or am I setting myself a challenge to which I cannot succeed?
>
> Yet I still go back, keep doing it, get excited, regroup, reframe, refresh my material and approach, learn and carry on. When I am given the opportunity to teach complexity again, I always jump at the challenge.'

If we are called to teach, then teach we must, in order to be fulfilled. Teaching as activism requires first of all, a thorough knowledge of, and love for, your topic. It demands courage to present your truth with integrity in a sceptical environment. Teaching also requires an ability to attend to many threads at once; to think quickly, adapt content and process to context, and develop the inner and outer resources needed to maintain the leadership that your experience, knowledge and wisdom (not just your job title) entitle you to hold. Yet for those who love it, nothing is more worthwhile.

Speak Out

At the top of a hill in Devon there is a fifteen-foot oak tree. In her position at the top of the hill, she looks not only south towards the sea, but north to Dartmoor. Often when I crest that hill, I'm instantly assailed by ice wind blowing straight from the moor, and I button myself into my jacket a little more snugly. The oak, though, stands there naked except for a little ivy. She speaks to the Trembling Warrior in me: exposed, vulnerable, but very much alive, and doing her thing. She reminds me of how I have sometimes felt when speaking in public.

Speaking out brings what Trembling Warriors care most about into the public discourse. When you speak out, your voice can change the narrative, or at least feed into it. Or... it can float away unheard. You can't know which of these has happened, regardless of whether those who hear you look rapturous or indifferent. You have no way of knowing what they carry away with them, consciously or otherwise, that might nudge the direction of the human story. So it's always worth adding your voice: whether in the classroom or conference room, political meeting or festival; or on a soap box in the street.

Ideally, we want the biggest possible audience for our message: if we can get a radio or TV interview, so much the better. Such a thought is likely to cast fear into a hedge-dweller's heart: for many, public speaking is terrifying - and understandably so. Even the most inclusive and compassionate audiences judge speakers swiftly and with alarming detachment, comparing assessments afterwards. To stand in front of an audience and speak, knowing how audiences judge speakers, takes courage - something Trembling Warriors don't possess in spades. Yet your inner preacher may compel you to do it anyway. You will be told to develop a thick skin, but if you are naturally tender, you may not be able to develop thick skin - or actually even want to. Sometimes it's easier to find the grace to know ourselves judged, and say what we need to say anyway.

Speaking in public isn't, of course, compulsory. You get to choose whether you're willing to take a risk or not: if you really don't want to, you really don't have to. For strong introverts, making videos to post online is a good way to get your message across. You can re-record and edit for as long as you like, until you're happy with what you've got – and if there are any comments or questions, you have plenty of time to reflect before responding. Also, if you receive any criticism, there's no-one to witness your response and recovery time. However, many Trembling Warriors are on fire when *we have explicit or implicit permission* to speak out. When we feel ourselves affirmed and welcomed, we can be eloquent, passionate, warm and persuasive. But if something happens to interrupt the exchange of expression and affirmation, that confidence can quickly shrivel. We suspect we're inadequate, and that those round us have noticed: that activates a threat response, shutting down our flow. Trembling is natural; audiences will forgive you that, as long as you speak with conviction. But if you bring an apologetic demeanour, you'll keep the attention of only the most polite audience members. You can learn to *look and sound* confident. But far better, build your sense of self-worth through some form of personal development work, and build your knowledge as a sure foundation.

It's wise to stick to speaking about what you know. Idealists, especially introverted ones, have great absorption and rich memory stores for wisdom related to our passions. Intuitives are generally able to talk easily and fluently about ideas, but can falter when asked for facts, which can make answering questions tricky. It helps to 'cram' facts beforehand: any relevant names, numbers and dates will probably stay in your head until at least after the event! In the public arena, we can feel under immense pressure to know everything, to perform perfectly, so as to avoid that debilitating emotion: shame. In a media-driven culture, we can feel disproportionate levels of shame for not knowing everything, not performing perfectly. And it's not lack of knowledge or poor performance itself, but the jeering, dismissal and belittling that can lead to feeling humiliated.

I have run numerous presentation skills courses, and I've seen fear of humiliation prevent good people from stepping up, and thwart them in doing and giving their best. I've also seen what people can do when they are supported and encouraged by the group: they surprise themselves and others, with both their knowledge and their delivery. Here are some techniques for Trembling Warriors.

- Prepare and practise. The better you know your content, the more easily it will come.

- Tell people where you're going; they like to know what to expect.

- You don't need to be formal, and cut your soul out: speak your heart.

- Limit facts. You may itch to put in everything 'people need to know', but they still won't remember more than a few points. So they may as well be important ones. You can always give out more detail on paper, or share a link.

- Bring humour: people like to be entertained, and laughter breaks tension for everyone, including you.

- Emphasise points you really want people to feel deeply, or remember

- Share examples to illustrate ideas: intuitive concepts can be too abstract for some.

- Take your time. Pause regularly for impact and to let people digest; breathe, and be present.

- Be mindful not to fix your gaze on someone you're comfortable with (or someone you're afraid of). Allow your gaze to meet with as many people as you can.

- Let your voice be your instrument: for example, low and slow for grave situations; higher and faster tends to energise and inspire.

- People will walk away carrying their last emotion in their hearts. So even if you're planning nothing except to wing it - at least plan a really powerful final sentence.

Inviting questions is good: it allows you to expand certain themes, and engage with your audience in a more spontaneous way. But intuitives with 360 vision may struggle with an instant response. Usually verbally fluent, some of us can become temporarily dumb when we're put on the spot about something meaningful. As we look inward for a response, it's as if we open a door to a richly furnished room, full of gradually accumulated objects, more redolent with meaning and connections than their appearance can possibly convey. Add the rich colours, texture, and subtle lighting of intuition, lending the scene soulful qualities that convey certain themes or values. How can you accurately convey all this? Which aspect should you speak about? Will you get a chance to explain or qualify a phrase that doesn't make sense on its own, or even worse, that on its own conveys an entirely different meaning to the one you are striving to express? No wonder we're occasionally speechless. Be okay with not knowing, and don't be afraid to say "I don't know," or "I'll need some time to think about that." But be over-apologetic; indeed, you may be surprised that anyone would imagine you do, or should, know straight away. When we apologise, we instantly make ourselves smaller. There are times when this is appropriate; in public speaking, most apologising simply diminishes our truth.

Today people are encouraged - trained - to be controlled and measured; not to bring emotion in to presentations, radio interviews and so on. More often than not, what we hear from leaders of public discourse is bland and colourless, in contrast to the expressiveness, eccentricity and unself-conscious emotion that until recently used to colour public speaking. Most of us still prefer a speaker who can move us in our TED talks, though, don't we? We're far more likely to remember - and act on - what someone says if they touch our souls. To speak with true power, let it come from the source of your passion: whether your pain, outrage, gratitude, excitement or joy - fired by the soul prompting that called you to speak in the first place. That's when people are enthralled: they know they're listening to the real thing.

Ask the Question

If you care about animal welfare, or workers' conditions, or water quality, you probably care about how your food, clothing, and cleaning and personal hygiene products are sourced and made. And if you care about that, you'll probably want to know what you're buying, eating, wearing and pouring down the drain doesn't have effects on Life that you wouldn't want. Here are some questions you might routinely ask caterers and retailers:

- Where was this made?
- Is this biodegradable?
- Is that recyclable?
- Is the chicken/pork free-range?
- Has this got eggs in it? Are they from free range hens?
- Where do you get your fish?
- Why do you still use plastic straws/bags/cutlery?
- Does this contain any toxic chemicals?
- Shall I close this door...?

Opportunities are unfortunately endless. I have a friend who nearly faints when I ask such questions: it's "just not what you do." But to me, *not* asking seems bizarre and inexplicable. Why would I pretend I don't care about needless carbon emissions when climate change is so close to the wire? And what business does anyone have selling products without knowing whether they're toxic? How weird is it to handle, cook, and sell meat, never even wondering whether you're working with the bodies of animals who've been healthy, comfortable and content, or pigs and hens whose miserable existence Juliet and Lars have worked so hard to expose? Something's gone badly wrong with the system when people whose work this is don't know the answers, or even understand the issues. Yet it happens everywhere, every day, partly because customers don't question it. Asking the question as daily activating can make a huge difference, yet Trembling Warriors refrain for several reasons.

I'm often challenged about the fact that a lot of people can't afford to purchase ethically. It's a good challenge, but the energy behind the accusations sometimes feels defensive. It's simply true that most people could afford at least some ethical alternatives: for example, a fresh organic veg box, a selection of beans and pulses, and some herbs or spices generally costs less than the equivalent number of ready meals, and DIY 'green cleaning' is cheaper than buying chemical products. Buying clothes from a charity shop does no harm, but the manufacture of most new clothes does.

Many people simply choose to prioritise their spending differently. Others simply have little sense of how their purchasing choices impact on Life. In *The Game*, I call this playing the Sleepwalker avatar. Many are aware at some level, but perform a disconnect between values and lifestyle in an attempt to maintain comfort (though once we know about the issues, we can never un-know, and that can lead to more inner tension than we realise.) I call this the Avoider avatar.

Many reluctant activists fear conflict because they find it disturbing. For some, asking a simple question about sourcing or sustainability comes naturally, but for others it brings up a host of concerns: Will I sound over-critical? Will they see me as interfering? Will other customers think I'm being unpleasant? Will someone attack me back? And, if I get an answer I don't like, will I have to make inconvenient personal commitments?

These concerns are real, but asking the question is a powerful way be effective every day in shifting society towards natural care for Life. When retailers or caterers know people care, they pay more attention to their sourcing. And how will they know people care, if no-one asks the question? In my experience, ethical questions are usually met with more puzzlement than anything else: "I've never been asked that before." Even if you genuinely can't afford an ethically sourced item, asking the question anyway helps to shift perceptions, and thus the system.

It's useful to ask questions even where ethical standards seem to be a given - and perhaps especially in such places. It's a sad fact that many companies which start out with high ethical standards and a vision, gradually lose both as they are lured by increasing efficiency and profit (or have to, to keep trading). Here are a couple of examples among thousands. Cornish clothing company Seasalt was known not only for its stripes, but for locally designed and garments, and their use of organic cotton. Over the years as they've expanded their range, fewer and fewer lines are organic, and more and more clothes are imported. Yet ethically aware clothes shoppers continue to trust the brand. I asked the question, and found that while there is a Corporate Social Responsibility Team working on ethical issues, compromises have been made as the company has grown.

The Venus seaside catering brand makes much of their ethical sourcing, and you can read on the tray liner about the benefits of eating organic meat. One morning I noticed the bread was different, and I wondered if it had additives I didn't want added. So I asked the question - about their bread, but also about their meat, while I was at it. The staff didn't have all the answers - only that the bacon and sausages arrived 'from a local butcher' (which guarantees nothing about welfare, unless you then speak to the butcher). I emailed my questions the proprietor: it's useful to raise issues where decisions are made. His response detailed a lot of genuine ethical sourcing, but was vague in places, so I requested clarification. I discovered that the bacon came from 'a factory outside the county', and they were currently looking at sourcing chicken from France, welfare standards unknown... A year later, I asked for an update. The chicken is local, and free range, but not organic. The bacon is not organic, and comes from pigs who've been industrially farmed - which you'd never guess from the tray liner.

Some of us are naturals at asking the question, as likely to tremble from anger as fear. Activist and mother of three Deb is one of them.

> "A fish and chip shop in my town changed from cardboard containers to Styrofoam, because they were cheaper. I asked the owner about the new containers. She said, 'No, they're not recyclable. You're the second person who's asked me that in the last ten minutes.' I felt a bit hypocritical that I got the fish and chips anyway, but I went away happy that I wasn't on my own; someone else had asked. It must have made a difference, because the next time I went in - with my own container, I might add - cardboard boxes were back."

If asking the question in public feels like a step too far, you might like to bring ethics up on review sites (these are normally very ego-centric, with a string focus on personal gratification, so you're culture-jamming too). Artist Jenna, who describes herself as conflict-averse, told me, "Whenever I saw a post on Facebook about a pub ditching plastic straws, I'd tag my local and ask politely and cheerfully, 'How about it?' Eventually they did stop using plastic straws, though it probably had more to do with Blue Planet than me."

On review sites you may feel the urge to hide behind online anonymity and express anger or frustration with retailers in a way that hurts or offends people. You may keep the issue in public awareness, and bring it to the attention of service providers, but will inevitably evoke defensiveness and resistance. Besides, for Trembling Warriors it's usually more congruent (as well as far more effective) to say what you liked about the service, and then explain clearly and respectfully what you'd like to see change, and why. Even if that one establishment doesn't change its behaviours, you're keeping ethics in the broader field. Challenging unethical practice doesn't have to be limited to shops or restaurants: we're surrounded every day people leaving engines running, dropping plastic wrappers, or laying into their dog for disobedience.

You can also question how people are treating their fellow human beings. If you encounter someone being bullied because they are trans, or Muslim, or disabled, for example, you *could* challenge the bully - but that may well inflame the situation, making things worse for everyone. A far more effective form of activating to is to engage in small talk with the one who's being bullied. Your supportive reaching out is likely to be reassuring and affirming for them, and also tends to defuse the aggression of the bully, breaking the 'bystander effect': that compelling group-think phenomenon where the power dynamic is accepted by everyone, even if they feel deeply uncomfortable about what's happening. It takes courage to over-ride the fear that gets us caught in the bystander effect: at a primal level we know that in aligning ourselves with 'victim', as we may become victim also. Yet if we are mindful enough to recognise what's happening, and have enough self-worth to reject the bully's power, it's a powerful martial arts-type strategy.

It's perverse and disturbing, but ubiquitous, that acting in support of Life is seen today as disruptive or unsocial behaviour. Most humans have simply forgotten that other species are our kin, and the planet our living home; rampant exploitation is unseen because it's 'normal'. We know that asking uncomfortable questions can make us vulnerable to ridicule, exclusion even or aggression. Perhaps that's why the Met Office was so cagey about climate change, David Attenborough kept largely quiet about environmental degradation for most of his broadcasting life, and millions didn't voice concerns about the rise of Hitler. That's why it's so essential to keep asking challenging questions, everywhere we go. We can't keep quiet and collude with the abuse: we need to change the narrative; create a new normal. If you want to make a difference: risk feeling a little uncomfortable, and ask the question. And keep looking beyond the corporate greenwash that you are bound to be met with: keep asking until you've got as close to the truth as you can get.

Have the Conversation

Activist Deb grew up in a Church of England family, and found it bewildering that no-one ever mentioned God. "If he was really all they said he was - and if people really believed in him - why did no-one ever mention him? I don't mean in a preachy sort of way, but just as a natural part of the conversation. You would, wouldn't you? I wonder a similar thing today: why do we talk, at home or at work, about what we hope to be doing in ten or twenty years? As if our disrupted climate isn't going to be shaping everything by then! In my youth I was the frustrated visionary, cutting through to the truth. I know some people think I'm naïve, and some probably think I'm on the autistic spectrum, when I shatter someone's carefully constructed and protected collusion." Deb often finds herself inviting others to dance to music they can't hear.

The Trembling Warrior is the one who dares to name the elephant in the room. Having the conversation - with family, friends, colleagues and in fact anyone you meet in the course of life - can be seen as calling someone's morals and behaviours into question (which of course it is). But doing so normalises talking about the aspects of global crisis that we absolutely must talk about, if we want to survive as a species: land use and species extinction; toxic chemicals in food, cleaning and beauty products, the carbon footprint of our daily lives. As people wake up to planetary crisis, they often want to know what they can do. Conversation gives more opportunity for dialogue than asking the question in a public space. It can lead to greater mutual understanding - or, it can lead to spiralling conflict. Particularly with family, we have a complex, loaded history, which often inflames things. Edwin explained: "I keep silent about my views, and don't engage with people who express views I find offensive (such as my racist mother-in-law). For me conflict has a very heavy toll and I 'hide my light under a bushel', yet recognise I am doing little to help anyone by being silent. I don't quite know the way out of it."

Edwin's silence in confrontational family situations, though, could be wiser than he thinks: trying to change others' values is a thankless mission. Environmental psychologist Renee Lertzman told Grist journalist Eve Andrews, "Our inability to manage feeling out of control leads to unproductive communication and behaviours, which centre around: 'How do I get you to care about what I care about?' 'How do I get you to change?' That simply brings up resistance."

Paul Hoggett of the Climate Psychology Alliance says something similar in an article on the CPA website:

> "If you're having a conversation with someone about climate change, the worst thing you can do is to go in with an agenda to change or influence them, it more or less guarantees that you'll fuck up. And we know this from the world of psychotherapy, that paradoxically, to be effective the psychotherapist needs to abandon her desire for the patient to change, to get better, and so on."

Most people are quite naturally afraid to truly consider the scale of species extinction, or to imagine real and imminent climate change (and implicitly their own death), or to let go of safe, familiar behaviours and beliefs. Such fear often shows up as ridicule, anger, or dismissal. I, and it helps to remember that, when we're tempted to get drawn in to arguing. Sometimes, a mild statement of disagreement is all that's needed to preserve the peace without compromising our own values.

Even more than most, a tender idealist doesn't want to hurt or shame others, split families, lose someone's friendship, or invite conflict. Besides, we hope for people to reconsider attitudes and behaviours, not entrench further. We can learn to engage in such conversations skilfully, but there are times when it's best not to have them at all. Sometimes, keeping your own counsel is the wisest strategy. But if holding back is a *habit*, it can cause problems. Recruitment consultant Gary describes an ongoing dilemma: 'Do I hold back, or do I share?' He described how he often withholds his personal views (especially at work) in order to preserve harmony - but his store of withheld emotion can come rushing out when a personal flashpoint gets triggered. Then he feels bad about his outburst – it 'feels magnified five times' – and dwells on it for a long time. Does that sound familiar? A mildly expressed response in the moment helps to allow your truth through without too much risk, even if it does bring your heart into your throat. And like anything: it gets easier with practise.

Habitually suppressing emotion that is arising – not allowing it bodily or vocal expression – has psychological and physiological effects. Watch Gabor Mate on YouTube for a wise and illuminating explanation of how turning anger inward can lead to all sorts of diseases, chiefly those of the immune system. It's good for us, for others, and for the biosphere, if we can learn to have conversations skilfully. Skilful conversations involve coming alongside people, rather than opposing them: find out whether they prefer facts and figures or emotion; detail or general themes. It's wise to guard your fire and reach out to others, trying to understand them as much as, or even more than, trying to be understood. Maybe tell them what frightens *you* in the dark hours, what you've only recently learned about, and the habits you're reluctant to let go of. That's much more relatable than pushing them to change, or laying guilt traps. Compare "You shouldn't be eating animals, because meat is murder" with "I was in tears when I found out what factory farmed animals' lives are like; I just can't touch meat any more."

Lars, the Marine who became a farm animal activist, had recently turned fifty-five when we spoke. He recognises that his approach has changed over the years.

> "At this time of life, I do activism differently. For example, I walked the Appalachian Trail. Everyone has a trail name, and I called myself Vegan. People would forever be asking me questions like where do I get my protein, and by the end of six months I knew all the questions, and had all the answers off by heart – and so did my hiking

companions! Hunting and fishing guys were interested in the positives of being vegan. I didn't fit their image of what a vegan should look like: I wasn't skinny, weak or pale. Some people were horrified when they heard about the realities of slaughterhouses: they just had no idea. These days it works better for me to talk one on one about veganism, and just to know that I've planted seeds, rather than scream at people, holding up a sign saying You Are Bad. I think as a person ages, they tend to mellow a bit in their reactions. I am now a very calm, spiritual person who teaches yoga."

Green Councillor Anna goes walking every month with the Ramblers, which sometimes offers opportunities to have the conversation.

"A lot of the walkers are apolitical, and I sometimes find myself challenged by comments they make. I try to find ways of breaking their prejudice without offending them. One rambler was complaining about people sleeping rough and begging. My friend and I looked at each other, wondering what to say. I mentioned that a large proportion of the homeless are ex-forces: people who have found it really difficult to integrate back into society. That suddenly changes things, for someone who thinks anyone who joins the forces must be okay."

When we love something, it's natural to judge those who harm it. But that doesn't usually help anyone or anything. It's fine to notice ourselves feeling judgmental, but even better if we can move beyond that. It may help to remember that we too have acted many times in ignorance or denial, and still sometimes do. It may also help to be mindful that some are naturally oriented more to the material and the short term, and some simply cannot perceive complexity, in the way that some cannot see certain colours. Shouting at them doesn't make them any more able to. 'Feeding frenzies' like the one we're seeing in the developed world today have always occurred, throughout nature, at times of perceived abundance. That's partly why so many ancient civilisations went on hedonistic sprees until they fell apart under their own accumulated weight. In the past, such civilisations were embedded within a healthy broader ecosystem, and could eventually recover. But today, our global ecosystem is unravelling under the strain of human endeavour, making recovery (for humans and many others) from an eventual collapse less and less easy. That's why it's so important for those who do see the bigger picture to keep finding *effective* ways of communicating the urgency to those as yet unable to sense our species' trajectory.

It's wise not to expect instant (or any) results from conversations, or feel frustrated if you don't 'win'. The majority of people, no matter how well-intentioned, intelligent or kind, need time to think about things, and need cumulative evidence before changing. Some simply don't adopt new behaviours until they're certain others are doing so. They just don't. Deb told me (somewhat energetically), "I was having a conversation with my mother about a local shop ditching plastics. 'Yes, all this about packaging is a new idea,' she said – even though I'd been talking to her about plastic packaging for more than twenty years." Her mother, it turned out, had felt 'pushed and pulled' by Deb about a topic that was simply off her radar. But she was more than willing to change once plastic reduction became 'a thing' – in fact, within a month of their conversation she'd booked someone to speak about plastics to her branch of the Townswomen's Guild.

Jim, who was passionately in favour of staying in the European Union, told how his views sometimes got him into conflict with others.

> "I used to get into heated discussions with my friends, who were all in favour of Brexit: in my view, not understanding the implications. One of them made a point about housing, and I instantly put up a counter-argument with no reference to actual facts - it came more

> from my values, and they weren't impressed. It didn't matter too much with them: they were old friends, and we're all used to bantering at cricket matches - particularly after a drink or two. But after several similar conversations with a former manager, he raised the fact that our differences were threatening our relationship. That really made me think. We were used to 1:1 meetings in which we talked openly and listened to one another, and this made it possible to have a different kind of conversation, where both we went more deeply into what really mattered to us."

Occasionally, a forcefully expressed, incredulous response to someone's unethical behaviour can be highly effective - even if we only get to witness the initial defensive response, and not the gradual cumulative acceptance. But our fellow humans are much more likely to listen to us when we truly listen to them, and when we find areas of commonality, finding and celebrating the things we all love. And if you can't remember the facts, send them a link...

To have the conversation effectively, you need courage, knowledge, patience, diplomacy, empathy, emotional intelligence, Zen-like calm, a view to the bigger picture, and non-attachment to outcomes rather than getting angry, or blaming the other, or becoming irrational in defence of your views. You need to develop good intuition for when to have the conversation and when to keep your own counsel - and equally, when to walk away from friendships that are more about habit than enduring affection or shared values. In both cases, you get to choose.

Once again, don't expect immediate rewards; none of us likes to lose face. If you want to see tangible results, look to the gradual shifts all around us in mainstream thinking. You have helped to shape these shifts.

A Trembling Warrior's Prayer

"May I be filled with loving kindness toward myself, and toward all other beings. May all beings be filled with loving kindness toward themselves, and toward all other beings."

PART THREE

Sustaining Activism

This section offers strategies and suggestions for *anyone* seeking a physically and emotionally healthy life, but focuses particularly on sensitive activists trying to stay resilient in a tough environment. It's intended as helpful and uplifting, but might evoke resistance for some. You may notice thoughts arising such as, *It's all very well, but I don't have time,* or, *It feels wrong to be so self-indulgent.* Juuso Jokiniemi is a Finnish biophile, activist and mindfulness teacher.

> "You might ask, why do I need to be kind to myself? Isn't this selfish? Or perhaps you feel that there is no time to take care of yourself when we have these terrifying global crises to attend to. This happened to me also. I was so serious and busy trying to save the world, that I basically did four jobs at the same time. I couldn't sustain it for very long, and burned out quickly. I had left myself completely out of the equation, like I wasn't part of the whole. This was a great teaching for me, which taught me that I have to balance compassion with loving kindness, appreciative joy and equanimity. My seriousness and constant hurrying blocked me from feeling joy and gratitude towards life which was not sustainable.
>
> Another very important and simple understanding related to our own well-being gets often easily

overlooked. If I don't feel well in my body, it affects how I see and relate to my external world. If I feel stress or anxiety, my responses will come from this place and take the form of these feelings. On the other hand, if I feel relaxed, steady and even joyful, that will shape my actions and how much possibilities and hope I can find in any given situation. Thus, taking care of myself first can shift my views of even the most difficult situations and bring resilience, positivity and hope for others around me.

Sustaining our work in activism, potentially over decades, can be extremely challenging. We need a lot of resilience, energy and determination for activist work. As activists we are full of compassion and empathy for other beings which are truly beautiful qualities. However, if we don't balance compassion with other supporting qualities, our life can get into imbalance and we can burn out quickly. So how can we bring more stability, balance and resilience into our work and life?"

If you are moved to serve the wellbeing of Life, that includes - and indeed starts with - your own body, and your own psyche. You are the life form you have primary personal responsibility for. Your amazing, complex body works constantly to balance itself, striving for optimum health. Bring the same awe and reverence to your body that you do to Gaia, who is engaged in exactly the same self-regulating process on a larger scale. You know the emotional health of humanity is essential, if we are to thrive on this planet. Bring the same wisdom to tending your own emotional life. If you're a sensitive idealist you are not only a Trembling Warrior but also a small, soft being, doing your best in a vast, complex and often harsh world, hoping to survive and thrive. Try bringing the same compassion and care to yourself that you bring to all small, soft beings who hope to survive and thrive.

Know Yourself

Socrates' time-honoured advice appears in various forms throughout this book. As with the fourteen forms of activism, the invitation once more is to know yourself, and trust what you're drawn to. For example, one activist friend sees psychotherapy as the height of self-indulgence, but is unashamed of taking time out to resource herself in practical ways.

We can, of course, never fully know ourselves. There are many hidden layers and tangles in the psyche, and the self keeps evolving and adapting, often out of our awareness. Knowing ourselves is a lifetime's work, never complete. I remember saying something similar to 22-year-old Charles, who replied, "I don't know whether to be really excited or really depressed about that!" However, it's a necessary process if we are to become adults and elders mature enough to be capable of offering true leadership. And on the way, it helps with knowing which forms of activism to engage with, and how and when to engage.

Edwin, whom we met earlier striving to balance an urgency about social justice with his conflict aversion, said "It's freeing to think of contributing in a way which is natural, and reminds me I'm better off writing and counselling than I would be in crowded protests or hairy direct action situations (both of which I've tried and find quite an ordeal)."

There is always more to learn: about our Achilles heel, our self-limiting beliefs, our strengths, fears, and our values and qualities, our unique gift to the world, our seeds of potential. It supports confidence: knowing what you have to offer and not being coy about it, and being aware of your limitations too. Knowing yourself opens up the possibility for self-acceptance; for permission to be who and what you are, and not who and what you're not, and have no wish to be.

Green Party activist Paula has become more aware of her inner 'woodcock'. "I was running here, there, and everywhere. Some people are like an arrow. They just say what they want, and they don't deviate. But I'm not like that. I try to be open-minded, but that means I'm often all over the place." Any open-minded activist amongst us might simply accept that's how we are, and fully inhabit our woodcock approach to life without apology. But we could also develop an ability to become 'more like an arrow' - *if we choose to.*

Leeann, from mid-West America, has been learning to deal with inner conflict around her spiritual beliefs.

> "I have at times struggled to confidently and non-anxiously assert my personal truths to others. I have at times feared the potential backlash against my identity, character, and truths—and even fearing the backlash that would make me doubts my own truth. That's where the trembling comes in. What has helped me with this is being solid in my identity and core truths. The more you are sure of your convictions, the less you are fearful of the impact the outside world has on you. You no longer expect others to validate your beliefs, or worry if they attack your truths because you are secure in them. For me, this has taken time and is a continual refinement process. It takes time to be sure of my truths, but when I am, I rely upon my conviction to propel me forward—even if I'm shaking or internally afraid."

When something causes you to doubt your own truth, you might try holding your beliefs in the palm of your hand, and examining them closely: get a sense of how they feel, sitting there in a clear, unshuttered light. You might grow more solid in your identity, as Leann has done; or you may find it's time to let some of them go.

I told someone I met at a conference that I was writing about Trembling Warriors. She said, "Oh, that's me." Diana told me she was a trustee for an educational charity. When she'd first joined there were two other women who'd been on the board for years, but as new trustees "with a more corporate background" arrived, these two were managed out via a "flashy spreadsheet" showing length of service in three year blocks: they were in the orange column, and they had to go. So they went, taking with them their enduring loyalty to the organisation, thorough knowledge of its history, their considerable experience and wisdom - and crucially, their attention to the wellbeing of the staff, and the land. Now, Diana (still in the blue column) was the only woman, and the 'new boys' had quickly formed sub-committees where sweeping business decisions were made. Her story will no doubt ring true for many women on boards and committees. As Muriel recognises, things have got much better - but in many circles masculine dominance, even when it's unconscious, presides.

"I do speak up when I feel strongly about the ethics of an issue, but I hate it," she told me. "Whenever I try to remind the board about values, why we exist, I get ignored. It wouldn't be so bad if they said *why* they disagree, but it's as if they just haven't heard me. There's someone I know feels the same way as me, but he just keeps quiet and looks at the floor. There's no point in me being there any more."

The next time I saw Diana, she'd resigned. She told me she'd suggested a meeting to discuss roles and purpose, but again she was ignored by 'the corporate guys'. She recognised that her context had evolved in a direction that led away from her own path, and she was no longer to make a valuable contribution. "There was no point losing sleep over it, and every point in channelling my skills and experience into somewhere more likely to make good use of them: doing something I actually enjoy. The whole resignation process felt like I was a failure, but looking back that's not true. It's sad, but the ethical culture, the reason I first wanted to be involved, isn't the same any more." She knew her values, and her limits, and when to walk away.

Do Something

We're often told that 'we can't control what happens to us, but we can choose how we react'. It sounds like wisdom - until we consider what's actually happening to us. Bureaucracy is extinguishing the flame of humanity, and the hungry greed of separation is sucking the life out of our beautiful, fragile, only, home. Why on Earth would we accept the neoliberal narrative, and train ourselves to be happy about it?

Trembling Warriors frequently find themselves caught in profound despair: about the sheer scale of harm to Life, our own inability to fix things, or what we see as others' refusal to understand or acknowledge the crises the world is facing. A great antidote for that personal despair is in acting: discharging the response evoked in you, feeling your agency.

Mac Macartney, launching his book *The Children's Fire* in Dartington's Great Hall, told a captivated audience, "You can do vastly more than you imagine you can." Trembling Warriors can find ourselves paralysed by inner conflict between resistance and fear, and it's a stressful place to be. But when we move through the tension and choose to do something - however small - we find we *can* affect what happens to us, even if we can't control things. We all have a contribution to make, each in our own way, to creating a new mainstream narrative. Creative acts of any form are so much more fulfilling than forever holding back. We can participate in campaigns that lead to changes in national policy; we can get directly involved in creation of 'new story' initiatives, or we can simply see and feel the effects of living in ways that respect our bodies and souls, as well as all other living beings.

Hurting inside my ribcage in response to the devastation of Devon's hedgerows, I tried to find out why such aggressive cutting was happening so I could protest it. But I couldn't find any answers. Eventually I plunged into research and blogging, action which at least shifted the accumulating trauma through, and helped raise awareness.

The impulse to do something proactive is healthy. But when we use action as a strategy for never facing our fear, rage and loss, we can burn out, stagnate or become disillusioned. Joanna Macy is the founding teacher of The Work that Reconnects, which offers a framework for shifting from post-industrial growth society to Life-enhancing civilisation. There are four stages to the work:

- Through gratitude we connect to our personal power and become more present to life.
- By honouring our pain for the world, the truth of our inter-existence is made real to us.
- Seeing with new eyes brings a fresh understanding of who we are and how we are related to each other and the universe.
- We begin to comprehend our own power to change and participate, as we go forth together to create a life-sustaining society.

All over the world, there are facilitators taking people skilfully through this process in powerful, supportive group settings, in a series of workshops named *Active Hope*, as is Joanna's book.

Artist Jenna tells me she doesn't get involved in activism. I ask her why; I know she cares very much about social and environmental justice. She replies, "Oh God, there's *so much to do*. Where do you even start? There's *so* much that needs doing." Her words may resonate. Luckily, you don't have to do it all. You *can't* do it all, so let go of any suggestion that you should. Instead, focus on forms of activism that energise you. What do you care passionately about, that you would choose to be in service of? What are the skills, qualities, knowledge and experience that make up your unique gift? What are you willing to try? What would bring you joy?

Paula, who had been active in the Green Party for many years, felt frustrated with several aspects of political activism.

> "I'd rather be doing something at a community level: something that has results, that actually brings me joy. There's just so much we can do at a personal level. People feel overwhelmed and think they can't do anything, but they can. Our whole day can be one of living in greater harmony within planetary boundaries, so we can practice active participation in healing, not exacerbating, the problems. There is ample evidence that what we eat, how we travel, what we buy and engage with make a difference: to personal health, community health, national health and global health. To be seen supporting good practice will normalise living within planetary means and encourage others. Walking, cycling, buying local produce, mending, growing, buying second-hand, refusing to use goods that are harmful: it's a journey we can all engage with. Our journeys are all different, but the dream destination is a vibrant viable planet.
>
> 'I have not always changed easily: for example, a man once read an article to me about the enormity of sanitary waste, and the availability of lifetime one-off solutions, such as the moon cup. I was indignant with anger: how dare he tread in such a personal area? But sure enough, my old friend guilt pricked me, and I explored the options and made my choice. For eight years after that, zero waste went to landfill. With all the changes I have personally made, I have never regretted any. They have all been beneficial in a multitude of ways. I'm not suggesting I am 'holier than thou', and some things will be easier than others. But the environment will only benefit from us actually becoming active in its protection. We just have to always keep that in mind."

Reluctant activists are often pleasantly surprised by the pleasure that can come from activism, in all its forms. They describe the satisfaction of having written a letter, the joy of connecting with others on the same path, or the reward of having helped bring about substantial positive change.

Comedian Maeve Higgins and former Irish president Mary Robinson made a series of podcasts called Mothers of Invention. They interviewed women from several continents doing something about climate change: whether through law, science, protest, or politics. Maeve spoke about the project on Radio 4's Woman's Hour.

> "Climate change didn't just happen accidentally: there are people who make money from it. But we're not interested in talking about climate deniers. We're saying, it's happening - who is helping to fix it? We interviewed indigenous women from the climate change front line around the world. They're usually seen as the victims, but actually, they're the ones leading the way. We met an indigenous Australian woman who had a background in science, and she's a river protector, as well as a midwife, and nurse. She's a really funny and jolly person, which you don't always associate with climate change. But talking to these women, I've found there's actually a lot of joy in the work. They're not paralysed by thinking about the scale of the problem, by thinking there's nothing they can do – they just get on and do something about it."

Extraverts, who naturally direct their energy outwards, tend to 'get on and do something about it' more readily than introverts. If you're a more introverted Trembling Warrior, you have choices. You could:

- Do nothing. If you choose a course of non-action, you'll need to give yourself full permission, otherwise inner conflict will probably rage on.

- Develop your extraversion. It may mean an uncomfortable stretch, but it's good soul work, leading to a more rounded and mature personality.

- Concentrate on something that plays to your preference: for example, therapy, writing or research, which are all very much needed.

Therapist and activist Paul Hoggett says most clients he sees in his consulting room are full of self-criticism, which can manifest in all sorts of shoulds. For reluctant activists, a strong and recurring narrative is about the 'shoulds' we impose on ourselves about 'doing something'. In his article for the Climate Psychology Alliance he writes: 'On the occasions when I've been involved in political action over the last forty years ... (Bosnia, Poll Tax, the Miners' Strike) my recollection is that I got involved because I felt I had to act. It simply seemed the right thing to do, almost like a force of necessity, a compulsion, was acting on me and through me.'

As psychotherapist and conference organiser Farhad Dalal put it in a lecture, "Discussing the state of the world without action or solutions is merely complaining, and all that does is reduce our spirits further." He might have added: action and solutions lift our spirits, give us hope, connect us with others, and *make a difference.*

Mindfulness Practice

There are three fundamental keys to *all* the personal resourcing strategies in this section. The first is discerning what supports you most effectively (and perhaps you already know something about that). The next is remembering to do them, and the third is doing them. None of these are easy when we're distracted by all there is to be done - especially if you're one of those Trembling Warriors who feels guilty about missing even a single opportunity to be of service.

How many times have you pushed yourself on a campaign or prolonged direct action, and recognised afterwards that you pushed yourself too far? How often do you allow yourself to fall unnecessarily into despair when you feel criticised, humiliated or rejected by the world's response to your activism?

We only learn from our experience when we pay attention to what's going on. When we are present enough to recognise the moment a familiar pattern begins to play out, we are able to choose a different course; when we're caught up in actions and interactions, we can forget to remember. Even when we're sitting quietly, lost in reverie about last week, tomorrow, or an ongoing piece of work, we can be pulled into self-critical or despairing thoughts before we know it. A good way to stay with our thoughts and actions, to notice them arising and make discerning choices, is to practise mindfulness. Mindfulness can turn all that follows in this section from nice ideas that you forget a few days after reading them, to real, solid practices that can lead to a richer experience of yourself and others, as well as effective work service of the broader world. Juuso Jokiniemi, founder of Helsinki Mindfulness, offers these thoughts on mindfulness for the reluctant activist.

> 'What we call mindfulness or simply awareness practice can offer us the foundation for our resilience, an intimate connection with our bodies and hearts, and a presence that is not so easily shaken. All resourcing skills are dependent on our capability of being present. If we are

not present, we can't consciously choose our actions and cultivate other beneficial skills. Instead, we'll drift more often into our habitual reactive patterns. These patterns involve unskilled qualities that our society supports such as over-criticism, aversion, worrying and the need for constant performance.

Practice can be divided into formal practice, meaning that we take off some time to practice sitting or moving meditation, and informal practice that we can practice throughout the day. Being present won't happen by itself, it needs continuous practice and remembering to come back to the present moment. It's important to explore what would be a kind and gentle way to reconnect with the present experience, rather than try to force ourselves to focus on the present. Including some playfulness can also be helpful, as this makes becoming present pleasant rather than a strenuous practice.

Coming back to our senses is the starting place for all practice. This is something that we can do anywhere: while eating, really taking time to taste the food or while showering, enjoying the warm water connecting with our bodies. Spending time in nature and connecting with all of our senses is one of the easiest ways to practice mindfulness because nature enchants us naturally. This helps us to let go of thoughts and to settle into the present moment.

One of the best ways to reconnect with the present is to befriend our breath. Seeing the breath as our old friend who has always been with us, taken care of us and provided us life can be really helpful. The practice becomes then to remember to check out how our old friend is doing and to linger with the breath and let it nourish us. Connecting with the Earth and our lower body can be another powerful way to anchor ourselves with the present. Tuning into the steady and stable feeling of the contact points with Earth can help us to feel more grounded and balanced. Another great way to tune into the present is to simply slow down the movements of the body, to exaggerate the slowness and in this way tune into the sensations of the body. Finally, what could be the most powerful method is to pause and stop all movement from time to time. In this space we can ask ourselves the question: "What is my experience right now?" From here we can start exploring our experience through body sensations, emotions and thoughts.

When we start taking time for ourselves and begin to sit still, connected to our bodies and hearts, our ability to hold more starts growing. We begin to build a foundation for resilience where we can rest in. This quality can be called equanimity. Equanimity helps us to be less reactive to the stimulus from the world that surrounds us and thus allows us to make wiser decisions. This space that we create for ourselves helps our body to switch from the sympathetic nervous system into the parasympathetic nervous system, which is responsible for the healing and regenerative functions of our body. In other words, our mindfulness practice helps us to relax and recover from stress. The spacious and relaxed space that our practice can create additionally helps our creativity to flow and gives us fresh ideas that we can use in our activist work.'

Mindfulness, then, can help directly in healing our minds and bodies: our whole selves. It can help to instil habits our minds and bodies appreciate and take comfort from: for example, fasting, getting up at a certain time, meditating, walking, or reading a book. It can also support us with engaging our *won't* power: the ability to refrain from hurtful words, a glass of wine too many, that extra hour on the internet; anything you'll likely regret later. It also helps with being present during a protest or action: focusing in a way that helps you balance your own needs with those of the greater good.

A strong part of XR culture is 'regen' time. Between swarmings onto London's busy crossings with banners and songs, teams gather for a moment to breathe, become centred, and check in with how they and each other are doing.

Mindfulness is a discipline, and as such takes effort to practice, but it is a habit worth getting into. The formal approach - having a regular time to sit and meditate every day - is likely to come more easily to those comfortable with routine. Others find it more effective to practice informal mindfulness whenever it occurs to them: mindful walking, mindful eating, and mindful interactions with other humans. The more often we do it, the more often we will do it, until mindfulness becomes simply a part of who and how we are in the world.

Self-care

It's common for Trembling Warriors to forget to look after themselves. Our passion for the things we're fighting for can take our attention away from vital day to day acts of physically tending to our own needs, such as exercise, rest, nourishment, and nurturing the mind/body connection.

Viva!'s CEO Juliet Gellatly has learned the importance of looking after herself.

> "I sustain myself by keeping mentally and physically fit. I know it's a cliché, but physical exercise really does help. I put in long hours; I work hard, but I play hard too. I know workaholics, and I see their state: they're extremely passionate about what they do, but working all hours without a break is not healthy for them, or their families, or even for the work."

Movement is essential, especially when it gets your heart racing, fills your lungs, and stretches your sinews. It boosts immune systems compromised by the existential stress of climate catastrophe and species extinction. It also releases endorphins, the body's natural pain soothers. They help with psychic pain as well as physical; and, the more exercise we get, the better we sleep.

If you are prone to worrying about the problems of the world, you may have trouble sleeping. There's plenty of advice to be found on sleep; here is some particularly pertinent for Trembling Warriors. It's good to avoid activism-related work at night: not only because you'll carry all that weightiness into the sanctuary of innocence that is sleep. It's now well known that the blue light emitted by screens suppresses a soporific hormone, whereas gradually increasing darkness invites sleep. Ideally, switch off all devices at least two hours before you go to bed. Before closing your eyes, try practising a meditation focusing on something you find calming: maybe compassion for yourself and all other beings; or drawing in peace and calm on the in-breath, and letting go of worry and anxiety on the out-breath. If you find it hard to do on your own, out of the numerous recorded mediations that exist, you'll soon find one to suit you. If you often find yourself waking sharply on full alert, you're probably suffering from underlying stress. There are many ways to deal with stress, but for the Trembling Warrior, it may help to work with a therapist and counsellor. This may not solve the world's problems, but could well enable you to engage with them in a more balanced way. Also, be aware that it can take as long as nine hours for the effects of caffeine to subside. It's a tempting (and for some, most enjoyable) energiser, but too much can leave highly sensitive people strung out and jittery – especially if you're already trying to carry the world on your shoulders. Try herbal teas such as chamomile, valerian and liquorice; or special soothing, relaxing or sleep-inducing blends.

We know, but can sometimes forget, the extent to which what we take into our bodies affects our emotional as well as physical wellbeing. Our culture doesn't support eating well – though that is changing (in some areas faster than others). In recent years a lot has been discovered about gut microbes, those little beings who do so much for our whole health when we look after them properly. The microbes in your gut are unique to you, which is why it's impossible for anyone to prescribe a diet that's right for everyone (and dangerous to try). But we do know that all gut microbes enjoy feeding on plenty of plant material, like plenty of diversity in their diet, and definitely don't like chemicals.

Yet despite emerging knowledge about gut microbes, and food that supports (or damages) emotional wellbeing, there is still a disturbing disconnect between the mainstream fields of medicine and food. A GP client told me that such a vital area is scarcely touched on in six years of training, and that it takes courage to address lifestyle choices such as diet and exercise with patients, in a profession where the accepted model (follow the money...) is to prescribe pharmaceutical products. Representatives from the food industry are usually present on panels developing health recommendations about food. That would be a wonderful thing, if their primary concern was health rather than profit: then they would be advocating food – real food – instead of synthetic chemicals that preserve shelf-life, add bulk, and so on. Meanwhile we might do well to take author Michael Pollan's advice: Eat Food. Not Too Much. Mostly Plants.

It's becoming increasingly easy to buy 'real food' that's synthetic-free, but it's always been possible to grow our own. Busy activists may not feel they have the time or inclination to grow veg, but even an hour or so in the garden every few days gives the body a good workout, allowing stress to move through. The physical activity can help bring a different perspective and fresh ideas, and having our hands in the soil and being amongst the birds is a tonic for the biophile's soul. The super-fresh food we get to harvest is a bonus; so is the reward of having grown it. Veg growing can be a good reminder of why we became activists in the first place, immersing us as it does in the rich process of life.

If you can't (or don't want to) grow food, you might like to forage for it. Moving freely around the land, and plucking our nourishment from it, is an ancient birth right humanity has sacrificed – partly because we're so numerous, and partly because the fundamental act of feeding ourselves has been outsourced, in an economy that monetises everything it can. Most of us pay someone else to feed us, to shelter us, and even to remove our waste. As we have seen, opting out of an outsourced life to reclaim the raw act of living is a powerful form of subversion.

Body therapist Sophia helps people pay attention to the mind/body connection.

> 'I see embodiment as a goal and a practice. We can all work towards becoming more embodied. But at the same time, it is also a given: we all have a body, we can disconnect from our experience but nevertheless it is still there, it is still happening whether we like it or not. Practising body awareness helps me stay grounded and helps to "get out of my head" when I feel stuck there. Trust is very important, I need to trust the process and

in a safe place let my body do what it needs to do: shake, move, make a sound etc. without judgement. We are nature and our bodies reconnect and re-mind us to that. Coming back to the breath in a gentle and kind way is also powerful. I know when my breathing is shallow that I'm not fully in touch with my experience. I used to have a supervisor who often and very gently asked: *"And if you breathe...?"* It's a question that has stayed with me and I use every day. It is so simple yet it can powerfully transform my experience.

Embodiment is a way of getting in touch both with our wisdom and strength and with how fragile and vulnerable we are. We need a lot of self-compassion and kindness on that path. As a woman, being embodied also means being tuned into my menstrual cycle. Living with it consciously provides a rhythm to my life and teaches me the same way as spending time in nature does. It puts me in touch with my strength and my vulnerability. It shows me that there is a time for everything, that everything passes, time and life are cyclical. There is time to expand my energies and go for what I want and there is time for letting go and to let things die. It teaches me to live with the seasons and cherish them. Unfortunately, capitalism doesn't think that way. But we always have choices, and even small changes can make a big difference.'

Delightful Things

The work we are called to isn't always a joyous flow. I have loved writing for fellow Trembling Warriors, but my last book *The Game* was exhausting and bankrupting work at several levels. I had to draw on my shadow qualities for a prolonged time to write for people unlike me, and sometimes I doubted that I should be doing it at all. Three times my ego self walked away from it, but three times the work called me back, and so I completed it. After a week of rest, I told my friend Kathy that I was ready for my next project. She wisely advised me to "Just do delightful things for a while." She was so right. We all have times when a week is nowhere near enough to replenish our reserves. But it can take several weeks of downtime even to see that. So I joined a relaxed, friendly singing group, visited friends, went for long spring walks, and then went to Norway with my partner for three months, where I enjoyed some blissful wilderness time. On returning I posted a new profile picture on Facebook, and someone commented she'd never seen me look so relaxed and happy. I told her what I'd been doing: washing socks in a bucket. It may not work for everyone, but it certainly did it for me...

Long-term activist Anna is clear about the place of pleasure in her life. "I enjoy the social aspect of activism; everyone likes to belong. But I don't want to spend all my time on 'causes'. I want to garden, write, walk, see films, see friends. I can't pack it all in! Anyway, these things energise me, so I'm better able to do other stuff. Just standing or sitting by the river for ten minutes makes me feel positive about the day ahead."

If you're a committed activist, you may find that even while you're doing things that were supposed to be delightful, your head is full of activism. It helps to discharge this: shake it out, write it out, draw it out, talk it out: whatever helps you to come back to a calm, still centre.

After years of being active on social media, in her community, and in the Green Party, Paula recognised that she was suffering from too much exposure to the toxic effects of soulless culture.

When we first talked about this, during the dark days of November, she'd only recently fully acknowledged that depression had become a serious issue: one she needed to address by being kind to herself.

> "This is very new to me. First I had to get past the guilt factor. Stepping back and practising self-care feels self-indulgent, but I'd got to the point where I wasn't functioning healthily. Depression was gripping me tightly. I'd become unable to make decisions, or find any joy or enthusiasm for new projects. I was going to bed with so much anxiety; my head was spinning from it all. I realised I was getting overloaded.
>
> So I've taken time out from the grind of work for a little while: so much work is not conducive to a positive and healthy daily life. I needed time to recharge. I haven't had a holiday in years, but just having time, even if at home, is so lovely: at last I can dive into the huge pile of books that haven't got enough creases in them yet. And although holidays are unlikely, the pleasure I get from walking or cycling in the countryside is enormous, as well as having the odd day or weekend away.
>
> I've started an online yoga course, forcing myself to keep to the daily schedule, and always feeling happy that I have done so. I'm also being conscious of what I eat: I've always preferred a healthy diet, but now I'm doubling up the effort. I've always had a spiritual inclination. I've started to re-explore that, as ultimately I strongly believe there's something out there greater than our material existence, and that brings comfort. Also, rather than being controlled by events, if I can't change things, I'm changing my perspective instead.
>
> Another thing that's helping is having the time to put my life in order. Before, I would always put my environmental work first, burning the midnight oil and

> neglecting self-care. I'm slowly doing my little home up: making it more pleasant, doing all those repairs, making curtains, and re-upholstering the chairs. In the small garden, I'm building raised beds and growing a variety of wonderfully scented herbs. I'm also tackling long overdue paperwork, ticking things off a list in my mind, and the stress is starting to wane. I hope and trust that strength will come back with a new maturity that will help me proceed with more clarity. It will be ongoing work, and I must find the discipline to keep to it. If we truly love, we care; and anything that attacks what we love is wounding. But finding ways to live with what we know is a must."

When we're so engaged with the consequences of what we know - and our responsibilities around them - Trembling Warriors with the preacher gene can get into a way of being extremely earnest; pious, even. We might forbid ourselves all 'unethical' pleasures in a punitive, puritanical way, and we forget to play. That's sad, because playfulness is a marvellous antidote to despair. I have a dear friend who shares my ardent love of wild life, as well as my distress about animal suffering. She also evokes my playful child. Whenever Janey and I get together (which is never often enough, as she lives in New Zealand) we share stories of joyful encounters with animals, and discuss examples of appalling cruelty and abuse. But we also pull outrageous faces at each other, laughing till we cry.

An essential part of self-care for activists is remembering to switch off - and as we have seen, not just remembering to, but *actually doing it.* Juliet Gellatly has cultivated the art, and encourages all activists to look after themselves. "It's important to take holidays, and spend time with your family, your friends - ideally time not talking about serious issues, but just relaxing and having fun." This precious kind of time out truly is a tonic: company and activities that refresh your soul, blowing a welcome warm, sweet wind through the corners where dark mould was starting to grow. You *know* the companions who restore your equanimity; you *know* the activities that bring you alive: whether a beautiful scented massage, or washing socks in a bucket; eating a Krispy Kreme donut, or taking a flight to see someone you've been longing to spend time with. Gift them to yourself – and if anything is blocking you from doing so, work with the blocks; with a coach, counsellor or therapist, if you're unable to get past them on your own.

But do keep an eye out for that moment when you feel yourself called back to work. If we become so self-indulgent that we forget how to tune in, we can miss 'the swinging gate' and slip deeper into habitual anaesthetics such as sleep, alcohol, drugs, sugar, or whatever; comforting and feeding our dissatisfaction. As with so many things it's a balance; a fine line to walk. Mindfulness meditation is an excellent way to be present enough to know whether yet more delightful things are still required, or whether it's time to re-engage. You might return to the same campaign, or the same form of artwork – but be prepared for the call to come from a new sphere: maybe one that feels more easily suited to your personality, and maybe, if your psyche thinks you're ready, something that will give you more of a stretch than you've ever had before. Neither is better or worse – except from the perspective of your deep eco-centric wisdom, that knows full well what you are ready for next.

Ebb and Flow

All humans, along with the rest of the biosphere, are subject to rhythms of ebb and flow. For example, when Trembling Warriors first fall in love with activism, we bring great energy: our wonderful flame. Then we realise it's more complex than we thought, and that we're not going to see change any time soon. A lot of activists become discouraged at this point. At such a stage in the journey, it can help to draw back, regroup, and then come back to the field with not only replenished energy, but a more informed and measured approach.

Managing your energy is a fine art. Extraverts thrive on varied interaction and a wide spread of groups and projects, but can become paralysed by all the options, or leave themselves no downtime at all. Introverts prefer to have less going on at any one time, working best when they can dive deep into research, for example. Both can benefit from the mindfulness to recognise *as soon* as things are getting too much (one early signal is the 'brain freeze' that can accompany stress), and then the discipline to put fences round inboxes, social media feeds, calendars and physical space, despite external pressure (real or imagined). Extraverts do this reluctantly, f at all. Introverts do it guiltily, perhaps because they see extravert activists involved in more than they are. When this simple human difference is understood and embraced, it isn't such a problem for introverts - or their extravert colleagues.

Sometimes Trembling Warriors immerse themselves fully in a time- and energy-consuming project such as running a campaign, organising a residential course, or putting on a stage production. We don't do things by halves, and for the duration of the project we're fully engaged: mulling it over in the shower, when we go to sleep, and when we wake up (and maybe when our beloved is trying to tell us something important...)

Full engagement in the flow of endeavour can be a glorious, fulfilling, time. But after the project often comes the crash: with nothing to engage us, we might fall into a slump and wonder, as one sensitive idealist put it, 'What's the point of me?' If this vital question remains unanswered, our sense of existential futility can grow, and we risk falling into depression.

If you're familiar with that rollercoaster pattern of soaring and diving you can, to an extent, prepare for the post-project slump you can sense just beyond the horizon, while you are feeling resourced and energised. For example, you might plan to get involved in something that will engage your time, and create purpose (but don't rush to put too much in your calendar: you may suddenly find you've swung too far, spread yourself too thin, and become paralysed). You can also plan in advance to avoid diving into any addictive behaviours that you know from experience will drag you down, and importantly, enlist the support of those close to you so that they'll know what's going on, and be better able to support you.

Whether or not rollercoasting is your pattern, most activists are prone to crashes resulting from disappointment and sheer exhaustion: in other words, burnout. Adam experienced three bereavements in a short time: his business partnership collapsed, his mother died, and the UK voted to leave the EU. The last was just as real a bereavement as the others: "I felt like I'd lost my country: not because of the economic impacts of leaving the EU, but because of all the xenophobia and intolerance of foreigners that's been unleashed. I realised how much I valued my identity as an EU citizen, as well as a British one."

After an initial period of deep grieving, Adam went on a journey, taking his electric car up through Scotland and all the way to Orkney, where he found profound nourishment for his soul. He returned with various creative responses to his situation, and one was to become "almost obsessive" about the Brexit process. He "followed every twist and turn", also diving into long technical papers, enabling him to challenge the government narrative that Brexit was inevitable.

He subsequently joined campaign group Devon for Europe, and involved himself in street stalls all over the county. "It's given me something to focus on, and a sense that a positive outcome is possible. And I've got to know the county better, too."

Campaigning was on balance a constructive experience for Adam, who had experienced periods of depression following his triple bereavement. He felt uplifted by collaborating with others towards a common goal, and was heartened and encouraged by people telling him they voted Leave, but had since changed their minds. As with Viva!, many thanked him and other volunteers for what they were doing. It wasn't all positive, though. "It's a deeply divisive topic, and things have turned nasty a few times. We've been threatened with violence, but that glimpse of the future as a nationalist country has strengthened our resolve all the more."

He wasn't always in the mood for campaigning, but he kept it up: "There are different roles on the stalls, and sometimes, I need to step back and let others do most of the talking."

In a time of prolonged national tension, Adam met with everything from optimism to aggression to plain apathy and resignation. "Campaigning has helped me stay out of the Remainer 'bubble' and understand better how people are feeling, what their concerns are. Although it's a scary time, it's exciting: every day there's something in the news that gives me greater hope."

An inherently optimistic nature can get us through such times, but sometimes, optimism can seem like a distant whimsy. Earlier we met Green activist Paula, who experienced a slump after a long period of active engagement.

> "The black dog days were far too frequent. First, I walked into a herbalist's shop to seek help. Another customer before me was asking for help with her symptoms. After a while she turned to me, and apologised for keeping me waiting. I replied, "I'll have what you're having!" and as we laughed, a third woman joined in. We may have all gone out with the same herbs to soothe and balance our systems... but the issues were far deeper than what herbal teas alone could remedy. Although they were of comfort, I could see no future, no joy, no hope. I was surviving, but not *living*, and it was making my loved ones worry.

Eventually I booked myself on the Active Hope course, based on the work of Joanna Macy and Chris Johnstone. It's seen as a gateway to transformation. One of the lovely souls hosting it must have spotted my need, and had reached out more than once to invite me. It was beautiful, and so supportive, and has taught me many skills - although I realised in the meetings that my depression was beyond even this. But it taught me to participate in my own recovery, and has given me many tools I can come back to time and again."

We've looked at ways to free yourself when you feel pulled down into the cave. But there are times in life when the greatest wisdom and the greatest courage lead to relinquishing yourself to a prolonged time in the cave: to stop resisting it, and simply allow it. When we experience burnout, sometimes the healthiest thing we can do - even if it terrifies us - is let go completely, allow ourselves to sink down into the ashes. (Human society may also need to sink into its own ashes in order to be reborn. This too is terrifying: we can't control whether it will be reborn, or what will be born: we can only wait and see.)

As Bill Plotkin explains in *Soulcraft*, we need the descent in order to be reborn, ready for the next phase. That call to descent may come at an inconvenient time, but if we don't heed it, we can do psychological harm to ourselves, as well as not contributing effectively; perhaps hampering the work at an energetic level.

There are often treasures in the dark. Your psyche may be ready for a significant rebirth, and that will take a lot of energy, leaving very little available on the surface. If you are called to descent, surrender to it as fully as you are able. Others may worry about you, or have judgments about you: you've lost it, or you should be getting out more. Or, people may even just forget you. Allow them to do that. Even you can't understand this mysterious process; most others certainly won't be able to. But don't go unsupported. You will need an anchor in the overworld, an oxygen supply as you dive deep; otherwise you could lose yourself completely. The provider of this thread of nourishment could be a particularly understanding partner, friend or family member, or a therapist, or a support group that may be the only thing you are willing to leave your cave for. Humans today are on a perpetual search for ways to make their lives happier, and society has all but forgotten how to support these dark times that are essential for psycho-spiritual growth toward true maturity. If you don't have personal guidance, you could do a lot worse than to resource yourself with Thomas Moore's classic *Dark Nights of the Soul.*

It's not always easy to discern between a call to deep cave time and a less healthy sense of hopelessness. Believing "I can't do anything" is a comforting position to take when we are afraid: it lets us off the hook. That's alright for a while: times come when we really do need to step back from it all, to replenish our souls. But at a crucial crossroads of humanity, we might feel we can't afford to be out of the picture for too long: just as long as we need. The better we know ourselves, the better we're able to recognise when we need to rest, and when it's time to step up again. Plenty of people will encourage you to take care of yourself; some will urge you back into action. Although only you can choose which is right for you, a therapist *who shares your values* can help. Core process therapy is one of several approaches that may resonate with the Trembling Warrior.

When you do decide you want to re-engage more than you want to rest, what do you need to replenish yourself? People suffering from depression are often advised to get out, get involved, and interact with others. Such a strategy tends to work best for extraverts, to kick-start their batteries again. It can work for introverts too, but select the nature of interaction carefully, to begin with: something you can leave easily if you need to. And remember: if you go to a public event it's alright - maybe it's even essential - to sit by a stream, or even in a toilet cubicle, during breaks. You can cheerfully disregard the mainstream narrative that you're socially awkward. Your psyche has so much to digest: people, environment, information, ideas - you may absolutely need some reflective space, even if that truth is inconvenient and unconventional. If it helps, take away the judgment and simply see yourself as a battery that needs recharging. It's alright – and maybe even essential – to come off social media for a while, or forever. When it overwhelms you, stress and depressive chemicals flood your body and affect your wellbeing. It's not only *as if* you've been poisoned: you need a detox.

Each story is different, unfolding with its unique pace. Standing for parliament and writing The Game – I can see with hindsight – were two very intense projects, one happening right after the other: both involving plenty of facts, extroverting, risk-taking, and disappointment. When they were both complete, a strong instinct insisted I withdraw my energy, and so I did: resigning from work with a client organisation, the directorship of a wildlife society, the trusteeship of a college, membership of my local Green party, some casual friendships, and presence on social media. I knew I needed a lifeline during this 'cave time', and so I maintained a few nourishing friendships, my one-to-one client work, and quarterly participation in a support group. Now and again, extrovert friends would complain about my protective 'bubble', and people would contact me with requests for participation. Usually responsive, I had to simply let them be disappointed. For a while I felt that maybe I had utterly failed; that any significant contribution I might have made was in the past. I explored some unresolved issues over four therapy sessions. During these two years I passed through menopause with relative ease, and this book emerged from, and into, my now spacious life.

Before the book was quite complete, I noticed my energy returning – with the wise timing of the soul rather than the intellect. My appetite for engagement with the outer world was back. I became involved with several Extinction Rebellion groups, stood as a District Council candidate for the local Green Party, resumed a director's role with the wildlife society, began working with another college, and promoted this book – carefully avoiding the mistakes I had made with the last one (rushing the finish, and not calling in skilled support at crucial times). This whole cycle was organic like any other process in nature: I could do nothing to speed it up or slow it down. All I could do was watch it, honour it, and ease its passage. And of course, the story hasn't ended: as I write, I'm in a phase of output – fruiting – that will last exactly as long as it lasts, and no longer.

Within the bigger patterns of ebb and flow, we all have daily, monthly, and annual cycles, that we do well to honour rather than resist. The tender activist is also susceptible to smaller ups and downs. With strong values often comes a pattern of rapidly changing emotions. Trembling Warriors can be knocked down by criticism, or rejection, or lack of response, or disappointment, but picked back up just as readily by affirmation, feeling appreciated, being thought of and included, or similar pleasant surprises. Meditation can help with remaining compassionately present through these ups and downs, and for many, they level out with increasing years.

Sometimes, you'll need cave time not because you're depressed or overwhelmed, but because you're deeply excited. You have a new piece of writing, or a song, or a picture that wants to emerge. Poet Mary Oliver advises, 'Creative work needs solitude. It needs concentration, without interruptions. It needs the whole sky to fly in, and no eye watching...' At times like this, the seclusion of the cave is what we crave, and is the most precious gift we can give ourselves. Such freedom may feel impossible. But is it worth asking your employer for a sabbatical? Or your family or friends to provide childcare? Or reinventing your life completely? What is your precious soul work worth, to you and the world?

Connection

As we've seen, Trembling Warriors sometimes feel rejected by society. And sometimes, they are. As Herman Hesse wrote: "Most men... have never tasted solitude.... they are never alone, they never commune with themselves. And when a solitary man crosses their path, they fear him and hate him like the plague; they fling stones at him and find no peace until they are far away from him. The air around him smells of stars, of cold stellar spaces; he lacks the soft warm fragrance of the home and hatchery."

But some searching inner exploration could show the sensitive idealist that sometimes it's *they* who do the rejecting. Borderlanders in particular can feel there's no-one else like them around; no-one who cares about the things they do. Introverted idealists often find there are few whose company they find inspiring and meaningful, and gently ignore the approaches of people with whom they don't feel a strong rapport. This can contribute to becoming somewhat isolated, especially if we haven't managed to 'find our tribe'. Even when we have a strong network, we sometimes leave it to others to come and find us; perhaps because we're away in a world of dreams or deep in some creative endeavour, or perhaps because we doubt our value to others, and need it proven. And sometimes we withdraw for cave time, either because we have found too much extraverting in social situations exhausting or bruising, or because we need clear head space to work. As we have seen, some cave time is good - even essential. But too much isolation can lead to depression, loss of confidence and frustration of meaning and purpose.

Authenticity and values are fundamentally important to idealists, and so we need meaningful connections with like-minded, or like-hearted, others. I worked with a gentle, artistic client whose family, school and then workplace were 'so dominated by a reductionist approach to life' that he had seldom met anyone who shared his values and interests. Despite having friends, family, colleagues and a partner, he spoke of feeling profoundly lonely, and didn't dare to dream of work that would better suit his gifts. My job satisfaction at being able to put him in touch with groups and events where he would 'find his tribe' was far greater than if I'd been able to make him a millionaire.

Meaningful connection can lead to joy, confidence, empowerment and agency. Climate protester Katherine was shocked by the heavy-handed law enforcement when she took part in her first direct action related to climate change.

> "I grew up seeing the police as protectors, and that's how I've experienced them in my work. So it was deeply alarming to find myself in a totally different relationship with the police force. I find it terrifying that police can be drafted in to protect corporate interests. I'm sure many of them have kids and want a future for them, but there are also some really unpleasant stories of undue force being used with some protesters."

Such experiences can be upsetting and traumatic. Katherine spoke of the difference it made, both at the time and since, to have a rich and supportive connection with like-minded others.

> "I would really encourage anyone who wants to get involved in direct action but feels uncertain, to reach out to groups who are already doing it – especially women, who haven't had a voice in the past, but now have the freedom to act. Activists often get high profile coverage and may seem like inaccessible groups, but you'll find them overwhelmingly friendly and welcoming. If there isn't a group near you, then start one. You could just start as a discussion group, and see where it goes from there.

My own experience of Extinction Rebellion echoes this: most people involved speak of feeling more at home, or better supported, or more joyfully connected, than they have done for a long time, if ever. Something magical happens when people cohere around an important cause with peaceful and loving intention. As grower Natalie Baker says: “I have just joined the Extinction Rebellion movement, and it was heart-warming and enlivening to see that I was amongst many others joining for the first time. I believe this movement holds one of the keys to broader systemic change, and we will see much more of it.”

Connecting with like-hearted others who ‘get’ us, and encourage us in our activism, can enrich us in endless ways. However, hanging out only with those who are like us can, of course, pull us into the comfort of the infamous ‘bubble’. As Juliet Gellatly, head of Viva! says, “It’s also important to mix with different types of people. It keeps you in touch with what mainstream society is actually like, what people think and believe.”

There are plenty more good reasons for connecting with those who aren’t like us: people of all varieties bring something important, that we not only are enriched by but can learn from. For example, the nurturers of society, naturally gifted in spotting and meeting practical needs, may have no particular desire to change the world. But they often act as a valuable ally for Trembling Warriors: supporting our endeavours in a range of practical ways, and providing a safe rock for us to swim back to when the waves get cold and choppy. They may not always understand what motivates us; it’s enough for them that we need their support. If we embrace them on that understanding, our beloved nurturing friends can be treasured and invaluable connections.

One tragedy that can be avoided is Trembling Warriors going into battle with each other. It can happen for many reasons, but such ruptures usually involve hurt feelings, and/or a perceived clash of ideals. Deb is a well-informed, articulate, dedicated climate change campaigner. “When I’m visiting family or friends, I can’t stop myself commenting on their leaky windows, or asking what roof insulation they’ve got – especially the ones who say they care about the environment. And if they tell me they’re taking a long-haul flight – or even worse, flying from one UK city to another – I can hardy bring myself to speak to them!"

She explained that for her, it's not only about the emissions, but also what she sees as hypocrisy. "How can they say they care about wildlife, when they go around in petrol-guzzling cars?" There was another factor she hadn't considered: her experience of personal betrayal. "I know it sounds stupid, but it's true – I do think, how can they do that, when they know how much I care about climate change? A part of me says, what kind of friend are they, if we're not on the same page about something so important?"

She told me about a serious rupture she'd recently had with a long-term friend. "I'd been trying to tone down my language, because people do get defensive. So when Liz told me she and her family of five were flying to Italy, instead of having a go at her directly, I shared a carbon footprint quiz to her Facebook page. She went mad! She unfriended me, and wouldn't answer my texts. I thought, okay, obviously you're feeling guilty and you don't like it. But eventually I missed her, and I asked if we could meet for coffee. I realised how much I would mind if she didn't agree to meeting – but luckily she did." After an awkward few minutes of pleasantries, Liz said, "Look, I'm still flying to Italy. Are you still able to be my friend, or not?"

Deb realised how "petulant and self-righteous" it would sound to say no – "and anyway, I didn't want to lose the friendship: we've known each other since we were this high. It felt like giving in, but I knew I had to. Then she told me she hadn't slept after the Facebook thing, and it had been building up for ages: every time I said something about emissions, she thought I was getting at her, but she didn't want to sound defensive. She said she doesn't like being 100% about anything, and though I do think that's often an excuse for lack of discipline, I know she sees things differently than I do. And to be fair, her carbon emissions are way below average anyway."

Two significant personality differences had interrupted the friends' relationship. Deb acknowledges that she sees anything less than 100% commitment as weak, whereas Liz sees it as adaptable. The two both care about the living world, but each feel called to serve a different aspect of it. "Liz said to me, 'I don't have a go at you when you tell me you've killed spiders or slugs.' I hadn't even realised it was a big thing for her. She never said."

Faced with the loss of a treasured and supportive friendship, and recognising there was a pattern in her life, Deb reflected on what she'd learned from the rupture. "There's three main things: we all see things differently, we've all got our own priorities, and it definitely helps to talk about it. Oh, and people hate being told they're wrong. But I already knew that."

Trembling Warriors have our work cut out as never before. Let's not fall out, or be scornful of those who are different in their priorities, or ways of doing activism. There's enough conflict in the world already, and our energy is needed for today's multiple crises. Let's nourish each other, cherish each other, support and appreciate each other, instead.

Support

As long as there is more to be done than people to do it, we may not always feel we have the luxury of choosing only the tasks we enjoy. If you are called out of your comfort zone, and then you're going to need some support. Good places to start might be Seeds for Change, a UK co-operative offering resources, information and training for activists in all fields, your local Extinction Rebellion group, or *This is not a Drill: An Extinction Rebellion Handbook.*

Seasoned campaigner Anna knows what comes naturally to her and what doesn't, but when it's needed, she takes on tasks outside her comfort zone. "If I'm daunted by a task, and know someone else who can do it with ease, I'll generally ask them for advice. For example, when I was canvassing for the Green Party, people who'd done it before helped me prepare an opening statement, to get the conversation going."

Emotional support is just as important as practical support: more, for some reluctant activists. Lecturer Rosie told how turning fifty had brought the confidence of worrying less about what people think of her. Age, though, can bring all sorts of emotional changes, and not all of them welcome. Muriel dedicated her working life to addressing social justice in the civil service. A lone female voice in what she describes as a deeply misogynistic culture, she pushed day after day and year after year for a more inclusive approach. She says she couldn't have achieved what she did without the help of one or two supportive colleagues. Eighty-seven at the time of our conversation, Muriel has continued to work for gender equality, and still mentors others.

> "Looking back over the years, I wonder if my 'trembling warrior' ran out of energy, determination or self-confidence at some point. In recent years, if my enthusiasm for helping, meeting needs or exploring issues meets barriers, I walk away reluctantly and devote my spare time to caring for my tiny, wildlife-friendly

> garden. Certainly the 'sensitive idealist' has become more sensitive and much less assertive in the last few years. My husband died after a three-year struggle: chemotherapy, and so on. He had been a massive support during my early days as an Equal Opportunities trainer. His death triggered a long-running bout of depression. I coped with my professional work reasonably assertively but in my personal life, my 'warrior' drive has been much more vulnerable."

When Trembling Warriors are supported and affirmed, they can be powerful, and achieve wonderful things that make a difference to many lives. But unsupported, the flame can flicker and go out all too easily. Giving support comes readily to sensitive idealists - as long as we aren't too preoccupied with our own story. Finding support isn't always straightforward: many Trembling Warriors are selective about whom they trust enough to be vulnerable with. Receiving support can be hard for those who tend to keep their vulnerability hidden from all but a few.

If we are missing key figures in our personal lives *and* find ourselves unsupported in our community, it can help to enlist some skilled services. Most of us find things shift when we're able to let go of what support *should* look like, and make good use of whatever shows up. Simply naming our vulnerability - whether to a therapist, counsellor, or a trusted friend, or within a support group - can begin to build resilience.

Trembling Warriors are most likely to find skilled practitioners who understand their love and despair for the biosphere amongst eco-therapists, eco-psychologists, shamanic practitioners, vision quest guides, transpersonal therapists and counsellors, and Jungians. The emerging field of Wild Therapy treats the psyche, the body, other living beings and the land itself as integral to such transitions. Take your time, if you need to, in finding the right person to work with. Most practitioners will gladly offer a free conversation, so that you can both feel whether you might work well together. Such intervention can help not only with building resilience and self-worth, but also addressing the anger and pain that might lead a Trembling Warrior to hurt others through aggressive direct action. Such pain is usually shut away somewhere safe, so you may not even know you're holding it - just that you feel vicious more often than you'd like to.

The Climate Psychology Alliance provides support for climate activists as well as people traumatised by predicted climate change scenarios. Co-founder Paul Hoggett finds that through therapy, activists can learn to be relaxed and joyful. "They bring the stresses and punitive fear of shame from our culture into the therapy room, where it is worked with and transformed, going back out into the world to help create a more relaxed, empowered and joyful society." For Paul, this "work with the inner Trump works with the outer Trump."

Groups for Trembling Warriors include Inner Transition (the 'hearts and minds' thread of the Transition Network); Active Hope and any other groups based on The Work that Reconnects; and Extinction Rebellion's Regen groups. These, and others like them, are supportive places where you can take your grief, rage, and trauma about the suffering of Life: express them, and have them witnessed and honoured, and shared. This is all the more important if you live amongst people who don't share your grief - or who share it, but prefer not to go there because it's too painful. But membership of *any* group where you feel at home - that feels like your tribe - is likely to nourish your sense of belonging and agency, whether it centres around meditation or making jam.

There are of course plenty of residential courses you can undertake to develop resilience. Those that best fit with the path of the Trembling Warrior include the Eco-Dharma Center in Spain, which provides respite and resourcing for activists; retreat centres that offer space for deep reflection and healing; Embercombe in the UK for developing courage and self-belief; and the Animas Institute in the US and worldwide, for a wide range of programmes designed for all stages of the biophile's journey through life. 31-year-old Borderlander Natalie found personal therapy to be immensely helpful. Her story will resonate with many Trembling Warriors.

> "Whilst I couldn't call myself an eco-warrior, I have felt the pulsing of mother earth come through me powerfully and take my breath away to the point of near panic attack. I think that learning breathing techniques is about the only thing that has stopped me having panic attacks sometimes. Even writing this email I feel moved to tears as I think about the times that I have felt the call and cry of pain from the natural world. I even believe that I heard it as a cry of a native American woman in Yosemite National Park, which was hard as no one else heard what I heard and yet it was clear as day for me. I know many people hear voices, I don't but I heard the call. I can feel very filled with sorrow and I'm sure that all the tears are not just my own. Sometimes it's as if I channel the emotions of others, like a conduit for emotions that I find hard to ignore.
>
> I realised in my 20s that I am a huge empath and that the dominant structure of the western world that we have grown up in is currently psychopathic. I have often felt completely depleted and overwhelmed as I have struggled to find my own boundaries. Often, I've felt that the bottom of my bucket of reserves has fallen out and can't find it in me to act in the ways I hope to do so to protect this world. This has led to me finding it difficult to go out sometimes, and particularly when I lived in London feeling very toxically overloaded and ill. I think that this is partly because I have grown up with the feeling that what hurts one hurts us all, and so have always found myself giving time and space to others and often being filled with them. I went to a great therapist in London who helped me outpour some of my feelings, and let the pressure out."

As we have seen, at certain times during our lives we find ourselves invited to face our fears; to dive into the shadow. There's no polite invitation – we simply find ourselves pulled down in to a place that feels bleak, chaotic and frightening, as our psyche is given a truly good shake. We have no way of knowing how, or even if, we'll emerge. Such transitions were traditionally supported by the elders in one's community, but when community has taken on a whole new meaning and true elders are all too rare, we need to find support where we can. We might call on our own inner elder, having developed that capacity in more stable 'upperworld' times. We can resource ourselves with good rich reading such as *Soulcraft* or *Dark Nights of the Soul,* and plunge into the fertile void alone. But such plunges into the underworld are held more safely, and integrated more successfully, when supported by those who have already made the journey.

Semi-Permeable Boundaries

For most Trembling Warriors, there's a tension between the lover's desire for harmony, and the preacher's need to point to a better possible world - which inevitably involves suggesting that others' lives could benefit from some changes. Naturally, such suggestions often evoke defensiveness, irritation or hostility. Sometimes these responses can remain unexpressed by those close to us who know we can be fragile, and don't want to hurt us: a dynamic we shouldn't abuse. It's far healthier to aim consciously for open and honest non-blaming dialogue, in which we overtly take personal responsibility and accountability for our views, and invite others to do so as well.

Trembling Warriors are often ridiculed for loving the wild: whether that love is manifest in defence of the wild spaces in your town, or your passionate expression of soul. Ridicule is often an unconscious defence against what's unfamiliar, and/or threatening in some way. Some people, from necessity, have had to repress their heartfelt emotions: their terror, their passion, their love. Small wonder that anything suggesting wildness (not being in control) is experienced as something to defend against. At a primal level, when we want to defend ourselves against something, it helps to feel we're bigger than it, and ridicule is a very effective way of making something smaller. Trembling Warriors can too easily allow ourselves to be made smaller: deferring to the Other as more powerful, accepting the subservient role someone assigns you in order to reduce your disruptive potential. But always, you have choice. What if you were to occupy your full space with the dignity appropriate to your visionary role; respond to another's defending ridicule with grounded internal compassion, rather than deference or humiliation?

Tender souls are often told, "You should grow a thicker skin." Thick skin, assuming we're capable of growing it, can protect us in many ways: it supports resilience, helping us to deal with rejection, disappointment and criticism. But if we desensitise ourselves too much, blocking our ears to what our senses or our dreams are telling us, we risk becoming less attuned to the cries of the Earth, and our creative work can grow dull. Growing a thick skin can also lead to disassociation. We may even become aware that we've shut down, become dead inside, without having noticed. It can take months, or even years, of therapy to recover our ability to fully experience our emotions.

Imagine a skin that's semi-permeable: able to let in that which is useful, and keep out that which is not; let out that which we need to, and keep in that which is best kept in. That's how our bodies interact with their environment, and so does each individual cell; and the psyche operates like this too.

I'm not suggesting we only let in that which doesn't hurt. Sometimes we have to fully experience the suffering of harsh criticism, or the sting of personal rejection, in order to learn and grow. You may even receive a clear if caring 'No' from your own community, at times when your direction is steered by fear, ego inflation, or lack of self-knowledge. Without these painful lessons we can't mature, and we don't reach our full potential or effectiveness. But we need mindful awareness and discernment to take what's useful, and dismiss (or at least park for now) that which doesn't feel helpful. Equally, we shouldn't allow in everything that makes us feel good. Compliments are like sugar: a little of the real stuff gives us good energy, but too much artificial sweetness leads to poor health, and addiction. It's all about finding balance. It helps to be mindful of the process, and aware of your growing edge.

A photographic journalist spoke of receiving 'brutal' feedback about her work, that nearly caused her to abandon a project when she had little time (or confidence) to start anything new. She tried the following activity.

1. Take a large piece of paper and some coloured crayons. Write down everything your critic has said, selecting a colour that feels right for each word or phrase, taking time to choose where on the paper to write it.

2. When you're done, briefly write or draw your immediate responses around each. Now put it on the wall, step back, and look at it as you would a picture in a gallery. What do you notice?

3. Now, return to the table with your sheet of paper. Let go of any 'shoulds': allow your intuition to guide you, even if it surprises you. You are going to choose what you want to do with each piece of feedback offered by this person, as you might sort through a box of things when moving house. What will you take out and use? What will you keep in the box, in case you might want it one day? What will you recycle, turning it into something useful? What do you know really belongs in the bin?

4. Finally, you could cut out each word or phrase and do the appropriate thing with it. Alternatively, you could draw hearts, boxes, arrows or bins round each word or phrase.

A while after completing the exercise, the photographer felt much clearer about what was 'true' for her and what was not. Her critic didn't know her well enough, she realised, to make some of the assumptions he'd made. Crucially, she found she was no longer hooked in to the feedback, having gently disentangled herself from it and laid it to rest, in order to do the work she believed in.

If your activism is visible, you will at some point be criticised. For a start, not everyone will like you, or your work. Also, those whose sensitivity is in their shadow might project it onto you, where they can safely belittle, attack or dismiss it. When we have a fragile or shaky sense of ourselves, criticism really matters. (In fact, it matters anyway: we're social beings.) If you're prone to self-doubt you might ask, Am I? naïve, weak, hypocritical and so on, instead of simply dismissing critical labels, as some might. You may, without realising you're doing it, accept all the words used about you, believing yourself to be everything – negative or positive – that others say you are. There is of course some truth in people's views: in one sense, you are what everyone says you are - *to them.* But if you accept all those definitions and allow them to shape your sense of self, your truth can get lost.

Sometimes, the boundaries we need to establish are practical ones, around our time, space and resources. Maria, a client in Washington DC, felt called to write about current affairs: to use her insight, accurate analysis of situations, and skill with words, to challenge corruption. Maria wasn't a trained journalist, having 'accidentally' entered a career in research chemistry. She regularly gave time, energy and money to support family members of all generations, and her career had never progressed. Now she found herself in debt and unable to pay for journalism training, let alone find time for it. She longed to write, and considered taking a part-time job so she could start a blog. Her priority, though, was getting out of debt - and she knew that if she didn't address the family dynamic, any extra time would be swallowed up. She decided to continue with full-time work, and use evenings to write. But she could only do it by agreeing clear boundaries with her family, making it clear that it was time to focus on herself. So ingrained and familiar was her servant role, she put the conversation off for nearly a year. When she did finally talk with her family, it was uncomfortable - but not nearly as cataclysmic as the imagined conversations. Hardest was maintaining her new boundaries until they'd 'set'. She had to give a lot of attention to those boundaries, which were constantly nibbled into and leaned against every day. Her family, alarmed by the change, knew the words that would challenge her: 'selfish... disappointed... mean.' But with support, she could step back and see a trajectory away from dependence to a more healthy relationship, and fulfilment of her potential.

Stepping back isn't easy, but most Trembling Warriors are particularly adept at seeing connections that others cannot see. You may, through meditative or reflective practice, be able to soften the focus on your ego: to gently let go of any personal hurts, and tap into your intuitive awareness about the path you need to be on.

IQ alone is no predictor of what someone will achieve, or how fulfilled they'll be. The field of emotional intelligence has shown that well-developed feeling is as essential as well-developed thinking. Classic emotional intelligence involves four areas: self-awareness, awareness of others, self-management and relationship management. However, Psychologist Malcolm Parlett points out that even with attention to emotional intelligence, we're still missing two important aspects of human experience: our context, and our bodies. In his book *Future Sense,* he proposes five dimensions, or 'explorations': Embodying, Self-Recognising, Inter-relating, Experimenting, Responding to the Situation. All are equally important, and none works in isolation from the others.

For example, Juuso Jokiniemi teaches mindfulness to develop emotional self-recognition, embodying, and inter-relating. The practice is an experiment - trying something and learning from it - and supports us in responding to any situation appropriately.

> 'Our culture has taught us that certain feelings are not okay to express or even to experience. As Joanna Macy says, we have to feel what we feel even if these emotions are so called 'negative emotions' such as despair, fear, anger or frustration, guilt and sorrow. Repressing these very powerful emotions requires a tremendous amount of energy which can drain and isolate us. When we allow ourselves to experience these feelings, we cease to fear them. We learn to turn them into strong solidarity with all beings.
>
> However, feeling these emotions can often times be very difficult, perhaps even overwhelming and if we don't have skills for this type of work it can lead us into a spiral where negative thoughts and emotions follow each other. This is where embodied practice can really help us. Embodied practices, such as focusing, enable us to slowly

reconnect with our body and emotions and to listen to their messages and inner wisdom. When we have our practice as an anchor, we have something solid to hold on to, which brings us stability when we begin to face the difficult. Embodied practice can give us the container, which can welcome and hold the difficult and let it move through us rather than getting stuck inside of us.

Emotional work can be supported greatly by groups and/or nature as we don't have to hold the difficult emotions individually, and learn that others experience these difficulties just like we do. This can start opening up a beautiful sense of connection and an experiential understanding of interconnectedness with all of life.

The beneficial qualities that we cultivate in our personal practice should also lead into better working environments because we are cultivating our communication and emotional skills.'

Whenever we fight for anything outside us, we are also fighting for something within. Even when we fight the word 'fighting', we are doing that. The better we are at self-recognising, the more we understand the source of our fire, and the more wisely we can direct our energy. Allowing our emotions through, with the right support or self-support, can be a creative and healing act. Activist Larch adds that emotions, when managed well, can provide powerful fuel for responding to our current global situation through activism.

"When we're fully and actively engaged in something we believe in, strong emotions can and do surface. We want and need those strong feelings. It's a matter of harnessing them; directing them into something constructive. We can develop a practice that allows us to be comfortable with all the emotions that come up. We don't have to worry about them, or fix them: we can just watch them and relax into them, and from that comes insight about

> what to do next. For example, if you're worrying about telling your parents you've joined an activist group, just relax and allow the worrying. Eventually you'll know what to do: whether it's choosing not to tell your parents, or doing something supportive for them as a form of action, or talking to them in a non-confrontational way that seeks their support and advice. Fear comes up for me when I contemplate letting go of two paid jobs, where I've built up wonderful teams and been very happy. That fear has been good to feel; it's actually been very empowering."

Emotions are with us all the time, changing from moment to moment. For example, when we encounter cruelty, we may feel fire rising. But as we mature, we can watch it rise, and then respond to the situation by following through with compassion for another's life circumstances that have seeded such cruelty. Embracing people in their wholeness, discerning without judging, we create conditions in which they can heal and grow. Embracing our own pain and immaturity, we enable our own growth.

Self-care arises from very different foundations in the 'alternative' world than in the mainstream. Big employers in the private and public sectors encourage, and sometimes even require, their staff to undergo resilience training. It's meant to help us cope with the mainstream workplace, and tends to be augmented with counselling, anti-depressants and alcohol. One way or another, we're required to take responsibility for our adapting ourselves to what may be an exploitative, damaging system: once we've done the training, a box can be ticked by HR to prove 'duty of care' should a court case arise. (Surely humanity is capable of better than this?)

I once led such courses. But over the years, as I grew in understanding, the courses became a bit maverick. I encouraged participants, before trying stress management techniques, and long before receiving a diagnosis and being prescribed medication, to address first *why* they were stressed. Such an approach, assuming the stress is primarily work-related, can involve pushing back against unmanageable workloads and meaningless targets; it might mean leaving, and inventing a more satisfying working life. Both are experiments, and require courage. The first approach may or may not lead to the second. Resilience, for Trembling Warriors, is needed for *challenging* or *rejecting* workplace practices that crush the soul out of humanity, not for *tolerating* them. I gather from several conversations since that this subversive approach spoke empoweringly to some trapped-feeling people.

A key task for activists working together is to experiment with ways of communicating that suit the group, engendering good inter-relating. Activist groups are often anarchic, rejecting all notions of hierarchical power structure. New, idealistic initiatives often declare that they will have no leader, genuinely intending this to be the case. Yet power imbalances (even though they fluctuate) are as inevitable in human beings as any other species. A natural leader emerges – perhaps more than one; but nobody dares voice the truth in what has been declared a leaderless group. The result is 'covert leadership'. Because it's not spoken about the role, even though it exists, bypasses evaluation and consensus – to say nothing of the tensions that bubble under the surface as resentment grows. There's nothing inherently wrong with leadership – only when power is clung to and misused. It's entirely appropriate that some people naturally take a lead. Indeed, others who prefer to follow may feel deeply uncomfortable and disoriented if there is no clear leadership.

Any activist group wishing to self-organise would do well to borrow from mainstream organisational development and human resources. There is much well-funded and thoroughly researched work on self-managing teams and emergent leadership – leadership that spontaneously comes from any member of the group in response to the situation, and is accepted by the group. Such a model is possible, but for effective inter-relating all members need well-developed whole intelligence, and superb communication skills.

Without an overt and well-managed power dynamic, activists can start trying to outdo each other. This can lead to bitter competition amongst those who measure commitment in terms of suffering, all trying to outdo each other in martyr-like behaviours such as not eating, not sleeping, and becoming cut off from their families. Occasionally, these are inevitable aspects of a long campaign. Instead of competing, we need to find ways to minimise stressful impact on ourselves and each other. Everyone should want everyone to avoid burnout: if not from compassion, then to keep activists active at a time when they're so desperately needed. Activism with good leadership, and with emotional intelligence – eco-centric rather than ego-centric – can bring rich and abundant self-realisation, inner peace, and a sense of belonging.

Another problem that can occur without good group process is the witch hunt: the scapegoating of one or more members of the group. Witch hunts make things spiral downward very quickly, not only for the victim but for everyone taking part. People become fearful as they anticipate with alarm the very behaviour they are meting out, should they be the next to fall foul of the covert leader. I've seen it often in my leadership work with organisations, and it creates a culture of fear, mistrust, suspicion, cynicism, poor performance and ultimately, bad results. We see it daily in politics; it's why so many of us have become so disillusioned. If a country's leaders lack in whole intelligence, why should we respect them, believe them, or take them seriously?

That isn't to suggest a 'no blame' culture is easily achieved; it would be naïve to think so. To create such a culture requires us all to recognise and withdraw our own projections of failure, and fear of shame, which are usually what lead to a person being singled out. When someone does make a mistake, we need to think long term: to see beyond any damage to the good work they'll do in the future – *if they get the right support*. Importantly, we need to resist the pernicious 'gang-blame' that can be so damaging. As Alicia Keys sang: 'We are here for all of us.'

Finally, if you find yourself trying to decide whether or not to feel offended by something a fellow activist (or in fact anyone) has said, done, or written – choose not to. You can be bigger than that: the world *needs* you to be bigger.

The Path of Growth

In *Soulcraft,* Bill Plotkin writes about the value of committing our unique gift to that greater good which I call Life, and he calls Mystery: 'Express your vow in writing, or sing it or dance it on a hilltop... Don't hold back! Let Mystery know you say Yes boldly, *despite your appreciation that being so bold will occasionally lead to humiliations...* necessary for transforming you into ever more effective shapes and semblances for embodying Soul' (my italics). He goes on to remind readers of the importance of following through on such vows: the hard slog that follows a moment of inspiration if it is to mean anything at all.

I stated earlier that the authentic, eco-centric leadership of the true elder is almost extinct in today's society, but it's showing signs of coming rapidly back from the brink. As well as engaging in the day-to-day work that enhances Life and challenges destruction, it's incumbent on Trembling Warriors to grow into the wisest elders we are able to be, the most appropriately educated for the unique gifts we each carry. First there is the factual learning: if you want to be an effective presence, you'll need to learn as much as you can about your field, and then stay on top of developments. We know idealists don't naturally gravitate towards facts, but we also know people who like, and even insist on, facts. Personal growth is of course essential too, and appeals more than fact-learning to most idealists.

In the mainstream, people typically go on courses to get qualifications, or improve chances of promotion. Dedicating yourself to social or environmental justice may mean you don't earn as much as some; yet you typically plough any savings back into your own growth. Idealists go on courses hoping to emerge wiser or more self-aware, more knowledgeable and connected in our field; we go to challenge ourselves, to immerse ourselves in community or connect with soul – whatever will equip us to fulfil our calling in the best way we can. For example, at Embercombe in Devon, you can learn from founder Mac Macartney and his colleagues how to speak out to great effect. Whatever the skills, experience, knowledge, or qualities you want to develop, there will be someone to help you do it. Most idealists have usually got at least one book on the go: to expand and challenge our understanding, fertilise our own ideas, and stay with developments in thinking. Counselling, coaching, therapy, workshops and other interactive personal development can lead to clearer awareness of your relationship with giving and receiving affirmation, an understanding of why you over-apologise, or insight into your patterns of relating. Self-acceptance helps transform troubling aspects of ourselves into something more healthy and constructive. Edwin, whom we've met before, found he was able to do just that.

> "I spent my teenage years and early twenties full of bitter anger against humans in all sorts of ways. It certainly damaged my ability to helpfully respond to the world, and my contempt would not have won anyone round. I think I wrote off the 'stupid masses' partly because the idea of meeting them where they were and commencing a dialogue seemed impossible then (and challenging now). I also had views that were very much not of the mainstream and was othered for that. I learnt to be silent, and that made me fester. It took a long time to develop my interpersonal skills..."

It troubled me for some years that despite a career in personal and professional development founded on a belief that people can change, I had a growing suspicion that 'we never really change'. And of course, both are true. We can grow exponentially in self-awareness, understanding of others, and appreciation of the mysteries of the universe. But running through all of us are the fault lines that shattered and then set in us when we were young. If we don't engage in personal growth, they impede us in our work (and make us seriously unhappy) throughout our lives. As we grow we meet them less frequently, and usually deal with them more skilfully, and bounce back from them more quickly. But they are part of our essence, and will never quite disappear. Knowing them well as lifelong house-mates, and offering them compassion rather than judgment, helps to defuse their destructive powers.

Trembling Warriors find their work enriched and animated by sharing ideas with similar-minded others. Indeed, precious connections and interactions kept a steady fire burning in the forge that produced this book. It's also useful to get critical feedback from friends who, knowing your sensitivity, are still willing to challenge you. But be careful: criticism of the wrong sort, or at the wrong time, can pour cold water on your flame, causing you at best to doubt your authentic voice, and at worst to lose confidence in your project completely. Ask those you feel safe with when the work feels tender; those who will give you a shake when it feels robust.

There was a time when I longed to be a *name* in the world of eco-centric change (although I would have hotly denied that at the time). Now, in my fifties, I'm pretty much cured of the aspiration to be a global thought leader. The transition from aspiration to dedication came as a gently humiliating relief. As we age (if all goes well) our energy gradually withdraws from the ego project, and seeks ways to serve the greater good, until ego's needs are secondary by quite a long way. Later in life, we may find ourselves simply aspiring to be as wise and skilful as we can: whether leading a campaign or writing a book, loving those around us or caring for the birds in our garden. Such a change can't be chosen, or decided upon. As with falling in love, we imagine it's happening to us many times before the real thing (true humility) arrives on its own. I noticed, rather than decided, that service is more important than image to me. Withdrawing from social media played a significant part in this shift. Yet I can still wobble – and my ego is still active. Ego is an essential part of our humanity: especially for young adults, it's organically natural to want to compete and acquire.

Sensitive idealists are dedicated to personal development: it's coded into our archetypal patterning. When we have to prioritise, we will usually forego clothes, or beautiful things for the home, so that we can afford a juicy-looking workshop that appears to be designed especially with us in mind. The right learning can indeed bring joy, inspiration, and deep human connection as well as knowledge and wisdom. However, if you find yourself spending all your money on courses but never being quite satisfied, it's probably time to ask some searching questions. For example, if your need for growth or healing can't be met in a classroom environment, it may be better addressed through 1:1 coaching, counselling or therapy. Or maybe you are experiencing a pull as your centre of gravity shifts, and will only be truly served by a skilfully held ritual transition to the next phase of your life. Or, it could be that you have now done so much learning that you are nearly ready to become the teacher, and start passing on wisdom and facilitating growth for the next generation.

Meanwhile, there are many workshops, groups and residential courses to help young people develop as healthy, soul-centric human beings. One example is Wildwise in Devon, UK (mentioned earlier by Jenna), where skilfully held programmes offer nature-based mentoring for teenage boys and girls, to support them on a courageous eco-centric path.

Solitary time in nature can be a priceless and powerful ally on the path of growth. Profoundly moved by Mac Macartney's talk when he launched *The Children's Fire,* I made a vow to rise at dawn every morning; to enact my own soul ritual in honour of the biosphere. There have been occasional mornings when I've regretted this vow, and others when my fulfilment of it has been tenuous, to say the least. But the evolving practice has provided a vital bedrock for my own path. When I began, I was drawn frequently to the vulnerable hilltop oak expressing how I can feel when I take a public stage. Yet as dawn grew earlier with each passing day, and I emerged from menopause, I found myself drawn more often to a group of poplars I'd barely noticed, amongst whom I found I could now stand tall (although short beside them) and take my place.

Strength in the Shadow

We all become more fully ourselves, more alive and complete, when we heal the aspects of ourselves that were wounded when we were children. Our infant psychological survival strategy was to banish to the shadows aspects of ourselves that were giving us trouble; that felt too painful or difficult to face. Just as different personalities have different qualities, so they also have different traits residing in the shadow. A traditionalist could harbour a disavowed inner scruffy hippie; a rejected shadow aspect of an adventurer could be fear or weakness.

Trembling Warrior shadows might include the judgmental part of us that wasn't welcome in the family; pride in our achievements, if we were shamed for being 'boastful'; or speaking truth to power if we were frequently reminded of our smallness to prevent us from getting too big. There are endless possible shadow qualities, and we all have our own unique collection.

There are shadow emotions too, such as rage, jealousy or spite. Juuso Jokiniemi, teacher of mindfulness and Earth-based meditative practice in Helsinki, says "So called negative emotions can feel so difficult, but if we can open up to them in a somatic way, allow ourselves an embodied experience of our emotions in a safe and healing space, they can have amazing transformational power."

Whether 'positive' or 'negative', our shadow aspects were split off at some point, and bundled away where they could do no harm. They aren't parts of us we know about and are ashamed of; rather parts we have no idea about, and would deny strenuously if someone suggested we were judgmental, boastful or powerful - or whatever traits evoke a strong reaction in you when you encounter them in others.

Yet others probably see and know these qualities in us: underground, they gain power, and now and again they come bursting out - especially in a stressful situation. We might encounter them in our dreams, appearing as a stern teacher we shrink from, a vain celebrity who repels us, or a dangerous warrior trying to break into our home.

Our shadow characters appear in dreams because they want our attention - they ask to be reclaimed, and made useful. And although we recoil from them, they all have the potential, if acknowledged and embraced, to play an important part in our activism: helping us to be more effective in the world, as well as rounding us out into truly mature adults.

The judgmental teacher, welcomed home, can morph into a wise elder able to impart eco-centric knowledge and wisdom. The vain celebrity, once acknowledged, can give help us feel pleasure in who we are and what we achieve, not to be so easily undermined. Letting go of a secretly over-inflated self-image leaves us less vulnerable, and many Trembling Warriors would like nothing more than to have our secret hungry ego fed - although our scruples may have us deny it strenuously. And the violent warrior, when let into the house, will usually go to work on our behalf: protecting our boundaries and fighting for what we love. And so on. Shadow aspects are usually from our less preferred functions: for example, an activist with strong feeling and undeveloped thinking has probably banished the hard logic they might use for planning strategy, having an effective argument, or being able to depersonalise projections in the form of harsh criticism.

When we project all the 'badness' on to others, our own flaws go unrecognised, or at least disowned. When we're able to withdraw some of those projections and embrace our own fallibility, not only do we become more integrated and adult, but we also find ourselves recognising and appreciating the good in humankind. We may reject arrogance, but we could use confidence. We may resent those who dominate discussions, but we need enough extraversion to have our voices heard. We may recoil from coldness, but sometimes a cool detached appraisal is exactly what we need. We are may be uncomfortable with control, but we could use some discipline. Mavericks have an uneasy relationship with discipline. To the free-spirited, it implies being restrained, constricted, *corrected.* It is there to limit your self-expression, curb your desires, and force you into behaviours that aren't authentic. It wants to stifle the wild heart of you, quench your fire. Some Trembling Warriors hate discipline because they've felt trammelled, in their days of greatest energy, by parental strictures. Others had the opposite, allowed so much freedom in childhood that meeting constraints feels hard, irksome or infuriating. When we experience discipline as an external force, something being done to us, we kick (although we learn that in certain cases it's wiser to submit; that all we achieve by kicking is bloodied toes.) But when we see it as a *tool,* discipline becomes something quite different: we choose when and how to wield discipline that comes from within, supporting us in carrying through on vows and commitments to others and ourselves.

Meeting our shadow aspects and bringing them home can be a lifetime's work-in-progress. There are always new insights to surface around how our way of being evolved from our innate personalities, and were shaped by our responses to childhood happenings. Trembling Warriors tend to be committed to the project of personal growth: willing and even eager to face painful memories, regrets and shadow aspects - even if with a thumping heart and a lump in the throat, fear and fascination at what we might find. But if we aren't truly ready, such inner delving can be dangerous: we need skilful guidance if we're to navigate the shadowlands successfully.

I had a client who was visibly excited when I mentioned the subject. She repeated 'the shadow' in a whisper, with a gleam in her eyes, and I could see she was romanticising it. The shadow isn't usually something we ride gloriously into on a black horse, brandishing a flaming torch. That's not what meeting and owning the shadow is like. It means recognising and owning those aspects of ourselves that humiliate or even disgust us. In practice it often means an indeterminate period of self-doubt, shame, regret, before we emerge more integrated, wise, and self-aware. And disappointingly (for heroic-myth-loving Trembling Warriors) encountering the Shadow can also be tedious, mundane, even shabby: more like a rainy city pavement than a deep mountain cavern.

Shadow work is best undertaken with a therapist who draws on soulful dreamwork, sub-personality dialogue, artwork, or guided visualisation. You could also meet shadow aspects on a fasting vision quest, or a ritual descent to soul such as those skilfully held at the Animas Valley Institute in the US, or Embercombe in Devon, UK. Bill Plotkin's *Wild Mind* gives an excellent introduction to shadow work, but you will need to read it from the beginning for it to make sense. The first section lays out the model in detail, but stick with it, and the rest of the book will gently and carefully open the door to shadow work.

A sensitive idealist about to run a conference session once told me she was going to give most of the time to group discussion: "I don't want too much of myself in it: that would just be ego." It came to me that I used to follow the same humble strategy when running workshops, with my power pushed firmly into the shadow – until I received feedback that "We'd like to hear more of you; that's why we're here." But I held back from sharing with her the memory that arisen, in case it sounded like bragging. Although her session went smoothly, it could have been more effective: some of us felt out of our depth in our discussion groups. Afterwards, I heard someone say, "I would have liked more input from her: she obviously knows a lot about it." Our experience is one of our gifts to the world.

Wilderness Wisdom

Biophiles don't need telling about the benefits of spending time in wild places. When we're not engaged in some intense creative project, or enjoying meaningful conversation with soulmates, it's where most of us would rather be. We delight in wilderness: it can speak to our hearts, nourish our souls, caress or excite our senses, enrich our work, and evoke our passion – and our courage. It's the wild many of us are working to protect: whether from carbon emissions, or the de-greening of urban spaces. Even so, it can be of value to remind ourselves of the replenishment, peace, and inspiration wild places bring.

Kara Moses is a biophile, activist, and writer, who facilitates the rewilding of places, people, and society. This is an extract from her beautiful essay *Wildwood*, in *Emergence* magazine.

> "During my years as an environmental activist, I saw only a world on fire: another fracking site opened, another airport expanded, another forest destroyed, another environmental law scrapped. I couldn't bear to stand by and do nothing, and so I fought. Protests, encampments, marches, time in jail cells, always a thousand more places to defend. In the endless firefighting, I forgot to tend to my own wild fire, the spark of love and hope that had once inspired me to act on the Earth's behalf. The gruelling years exacted steep payment, and the spark slowly extinguished, vanishing into the surrounding dark. For several years I had been unable to find my way back to activism. Eventually, whether by intuition or by some unarticulated question, I came instead to Białowieża, to the forest."

Kara goes on to tell a magnificent tale of bison, wolves, and enormous, ancient trees, leading us back to the Welsh valley she's rewilding with renewed passion. Frequent time in wild places isn't just useful: it's vital. But we can get so caught up in the affairs of humans that we forget the wild that is always there waiting for us. We may sometimes despair, and retreat into our cave, keeping ourselves from a rich source of renewal. Or it can seem like too much effort to reconnect with wilderness: it is very hard to find somewhere untouched by the noise and pollution of humans. In most industrialised countries, land has been exploited in the name of efficiency until almost the only wild places left are marginal: coastlines, steep valleys, marshes estuaries, mountains, that people haven't been able to exploit.

Once, the calls of birds and the beating wings of vast flocks, and the cries of animals and the thundering feet of vast herds, the wind roaring through forests, earth-slides and eruptions, waterfalls, waves, and rainfall made up the world's soundscape. Some were familiar; others portentous. Now, these voices - along with the spontaneous, collective music and song of ordinary people - have long been usurped, robbed of their significance. Today, we're attuned mostly to the human sounds that come to us electronically, with a backdrop hum of traffic, and household or garden appliances. When the attention of our ears is caught, it is by strident garden machinery, the whine of mopeds, the buzz of light air traffic, the roar of jets, and the thudding of blast mining - or bombs.

If you feel starved of wilderness, cramped and stifled by what story-teller Martin Shaw sometimes calls 'the rinky-dink world', go out before dawn. At this liminal time, before humans have reasserted their dominance over the rest of the biosphere for another day, it belongs to the wild beings. There's a good chance you'll get glimpses, hear whispers, feel the fleeting but seductive tug of the other-than-human realm. In high summer, you'll have several hours of undisturbed daylight, moving amongst creatures more relaxed than they are during human-hours. But move softly: wild creatures have been squeezed right to the margins, and they don't have much left. This is their time. We are more blessed than we know that they are still here at all.

Around the spring and autumn solstices, dawn walks begin in the wild world and end in the human world, and that very palpable transition can be profoundly enriching. At these crepuscular times the air is full of birds' morning calls, the rush of wings as they move urgently on some mysterious purpose: whether a ragged V of honking geese, or a flock of finches bouncing across the rooftops. In the winter months, 'otherness' can be felt by going out before the sun rises; especially on those cold mornings when stars are still riding high, or you come suddenly into the aweing presence of the moon. If you live somewhere pervaded by the noise, light, and speed of humans at all hours, you can still find an experience of wilderness: in the clouds, in the bark of a tree, and on windy days when the persistent drone of humans is blown away.

Wild doesn't (necessarily) mean dangerous or out of control. It means undomesticated: free to move and express spontaneously, bodies and souls responding intuitively and naturally to their context. It's the part of us that experiences connection with all other beings, and so instinctively recoils from doing harm, and seeks to protect life and health for all. Being your animal self – responding to urges to howl at a rising moon or a devastated landscape, to dance to birdsong, to give voice to the music that arises as you walk down the street, to run not because you're late, but because you have wings on your heels: all are acts suppressed by a culture afraid of the Wild. When we give ourselves full permission to cultivate and express the animal part of ourselves, we contribute to a culture becoming not only life-sustaining, but life-enhancing. There is so much richness waiting to be reclaimed: abundant joy, power and fulfilment in a humanity reunited with its animal self. As poet Mary Oliver wrote: 'You only have to let the soft animal of your body love what it loves'.

Young activist Tara recommends body psychotherapy as a way of rewilding ourselves.

> 'I understand the current crisis as "disconnection" - both from nature and from ourselves, from nature within us. Our ability as human beings to disconnect from our bodies has helped us to survive, but it also enables us to cause horrible damage without realising what we are

doing. There is a need to reconnect to nature not just 'out there' but inside us too. Besides all the joy both can bring, this also connects us with pain, anger, fear, despair and so on, that can be difficult to bear. We can feel these when we face what is happening to the Earth; we can also feel them when we get in touch with our bodies, and through that with our unresolved issues and trauma. A lot of what we do to the Earth we do to our bodies as well. We can treat both as sentient beings instead of resources to be used and abused.

It's about trusting the process, the Life-force inside us - and that can mean going against what we've been taught we should do in a crisis: for example, the popular myth of the (male) hero in our culture, who single-handedly fights and wins against evil, or the culture of having to keep it together and be tough, might not be the most helpful ways of dealing with the current situation. I don't promote inaction. I have a lot of respect for people who are on the front line of activism and am really grateful for their work. What I mean is that we all need to listen carefully and trust what it is that wants to come alive through each of us.

On a spiritual level, I see the crisis as an invitation to more fully become who we are meant to be: to learn to hold the contradiction of interdependence with all living beings, and at the same time individuating and developing our unique gifts. Our ability to disconnect has evolved with us - so in a sense that is natural too. Survival might not be the ultimate goal here. Just as in our personal lives, the biggest tragedies can turn out to be our greatest blessings as well. They transform us, they break our hearts open, they teach us what truly matters and that death is not the enemy, but part of life."

So much of today's innovation lacks beauty, magic or life-enhancing properties. The fierce creativity of our animal selves has been suppressed by a highly rational culture, so we are misled about what's worth doing, and how it could be done. Bringing our animal self joyfully into creativity, without fear, we can create bold, beautiful and exactly appropriate contributions to Life, engendering a society in which humanity and the rest of the biosphere are mutually enhancing in ways never yet seen. Therefore, wildness is one of the most important forms of activism there is.

Mindfulness teacher Juuso writes of the importance of celebration: 'Joy and gratitude are crucial ingredients for us because they bring us energy and make us alive. We still have an abundance of beautiful things to be grateful for, we just have to remember to notice them, practice gratitude and allow ourselves to enjoy them.'

The Green Party's Natalie Bennett, in her article for *Resurgence*, describes a celebration of Life at the Preston New Road fracking site: 'an image woven into a security fence of what the fracking field could look like without the drilling rig: trees, green fields and a rainbow of hope ... Such creativity, beauty, play, joy are crucial to a successful protest movement ... and that vision of a liveable planet, with people living in security and justice, is one that is only available to our 'side'. Defenders of the status quo can only oppose change, not celebrate the unstable, dangerous mess their system has created.'

To celebrate the end of this book, here are some of the people you've met sharing what celebration means to them...

Therapist and rewilder Helen Allman: "For me, celebrating is cooking good food for people I love, dancing to music that makes my body tingle, and breathing in my surroundings when I'm in a green place full of trees. I would like to remember to do all of these things more often, because it strikes me that simply being here, and having the capacity for love, is always worth celebrating."

Complexity lecturer and 'flatpack councillor' Jean: 'I am happiest when writing or researching or pulling together a presentation - the deep immersion, lost in time, finding my brain still has the ability to find patterns and make unusual leaps. It is when I feel most competent, most skilful, and I celebrate this gift of creativity. And then nature, always there, always welcoming, giving me a place where I feel I belong, without qualification. And I celebrate my health and vitality and ability to find interest in most things. And those connections you make with some people that confirm that it is all worth the struggle.'

Grower Natalie Baker: "I celebrate the passing of the seasons and its cycles of sunny warm humming vibrancy and inner deep diving slumber. I celebrate the fertile composting regenerative power our earth and all its plants, worms, and creatures hold. I celebrate the whistling brisk winds of change and the tinkling rushing musical melody of the water that gives us life. I celebrate the powerful burning heat of a well-stoked fire and I celebrate the spirit connection that binds us all."

Passivhaus expert and Brexit campaigner Adam: "I don't really do 'exuberant' celebration: I didn't grow up with it, but I want to get better at celebrating achievement. I feel it's important to celebrate my son's important milestones. A lot of noise and high spirits feels a bit over the top for me; it feels forced, inauthentic. I have celebrated achievements such as my book (*The Passivhaus Handbook*) but in a quiet, reflective way. Annual celebrations like birthdays tend to be more of a pause, a marker, than a big party."

Anna Lunk, long-term activist: "Every time I walk down to the river and sit and watch - and feel so very privileged to be there - might be termed a celebration of where I live. When I walk with Ramblers through Devon's lovely countryside and along the coast - that's a kind of celebration of community. So walking either by myself, with a friend, or as part of a group is somewhere close to what I might term a celebration. And our little meditation group - sharing the silence, feeling comfortable with each other, that too is a kind of celebration - of community, of the place, of the moment..."

Glenn Edney, ocean ecologist and writer: "For me, celebration comes as a deep sense of satisfaction and gratitude when I have the opportunity to share my insights, learnings and experiences. Sometimes these opportunities come as a result of someone reading and being inspired by my books and making contact directly with me. These conversations have inspired me to further develop my oral story telling skills, which has opened up so many more opportunities to celebrate our existence within this beautiful web of life. What better affirmation of the value my work could I ask for?"

Climate activist Deb: "To be honest, I don't see much in the world to celebrate at the moment. I'll celebrate if we meet global emissions targets, or if fracking is banned for good, or if we get another Green MP (or proportional representation, which is the only way that's going to happen). At a personal level, I'm quite a hedonist celebrant. I like soaking in a hot bath with a glass of wine and a play on the radio, or cooking elaborate dishes for family celebrations, or dressing up in lovely colours and fabrics for a special evening of music or theatre."

Helsinki Mindfulness founder Juuso Jokiniemi: "My way of celebrating begins with giving thanks to the land, to the people, the more-than-human world and whatever else that I'm celebrating with. Then it moves into listening to my body and becoming receptive to what wants to emerge. Maybe it's a dance, a song, a story, a painting or a poem perhaps a mixture of all of these together with my dearest friends who I share this beautiful journey of life with."

Counsellor Anne: "If something's gone well, for me or for someone else, I put on some loud music and annoy the neighbours for a few minutes, and I dance. I use music a lot for celebrations; different types of music for different occasions. I often say a prayer of gratitude for what I've got: just simple things like food, and a roof over my head. And I don't know if this is celebrating, but when I watch my grandchildren and great-grandchildren playing together - they can't talk, but they're communicating with each other in their way - I hop and skip a little bit inside."

Trainee therapist Edwin:

1. When people are acceptant towards their thoughts, feelings and intuitions, when they respect their embodied experiencing as a human organism, a next step for them can emerge which is trustworthy, wise and pro-social. People are incredibly wise when they learn to listen to themselves.

2. There is a still point within all of us that is utterly at peace and beyond suffering, and we all have the capacity to maintain nurturing contact with it through spending time in healing silence. The more we do so, the more we help others.

3. While it can be productive to feel complicit in the earth's destruction, most of the damage is the fault of a few greedy people. If we occasionally pause to consider that, we may also observe that all around us people care deeply and want to help.

Therapist and poet Klara Papp: 'I celebrate being alive and embodied, walking on Earth, feeling, sensing and thinking deeply. I celebrate love and friendship in all its forms, connections with both humans and other-than-humans. I celebrate kindness and compassion and bravery. The courage to speak up and the courage to be our unique selves and do our work quietly without recognition. I celebrate the journey we are on, our ability to grow and develop and the magic of the present moment with all its richness.'

And me: I celebrate significant life moments over a good meal with those I love and who love me. I celebrate changes like plastics becoming taboo, and climate change being acknowledged, and Extinction Rebellion, and all those doing beautiful, Life-enhancing work of all sorts and scale. I celebrate when I hear dunnocks singing their spring song, or see low sunlight on tree trunks, or encounter a glorious flower meadow. Sometimes I just stretch out my arms, and feel myself smiling. Whatever else is going on, I celebrate that every day, Life still happens.

A Trembling Warrior's Meditation

'... quickly the image shifted into a larger perception where there were dark conditions/events/light and white conditions/events/light. All the time the dark was taking over the light and vice versa, constant change. I realised that this was a representation of the dark and light forces in the human realm, events that are happening all the time. Good and bad deeds, actions, choices, events. 'I' asked, 'What would happen if light took over the dark and there was only light left?' The answer came that this realm would disappear, because such a thing would negate the duality of the realm.'

Anon.

CONCLUSION

"A thing is right when it tends to preserve the integrity, stability and beauty of the biotic community. It is wrong when it tends otherwise." - Aldo Leopold

There is a staggering diversity of wrong in the world today: so very much all around us every day, that to imagine life without exploitation has become almost impossible. Of all that the domination of the rational mind has expelled, soul is perhaps the most grievous and serious loss. Soul is the deep, unique essence of each of us: natural, wild, and mysterious. From it springs humanity, joy in beauty, and ardent love of Life. Severed from the source of innate collective wisdom, no wonder we walk around unwittingly harming Life every day as we shop, clean, cook, garden, travel and work. Soul is not always pretty, but it is at the source of our inter-relatedness with the living world, and without it we are truly lost.

Trembling Warriors are here to nurture awareness of soul, and to help preserve the integrity, stability and beauty of the biotic community - even though doing so is sometimes far from comfortable work. In past times of peace, sensitive idealists have been able to follow their calling of visionary healer: whether in the pulpit or the monastery, the healing room or the hut at the edge of the forest, or the writer's Parisian garret. But today, bucolic peace seems like a distant, impossible fantasy. In the last few hundred years, distant wars and catastrophes have been brought in newspapers to our doorsteps, and recent decades into every room of our homes; in a future of biochips they will possibly be uploaded to our brains. We can't ignore the suffering, even when it's far from where we are. At times like these, across history, visionary idealists have felt themselves called on to cast aside their quills, their herbs, or their mystical runes; to leave their sacred place and stand, trembling, alongside the true warriors. One of our tasks today may be to support ourselves and each other in allowing our shadow warrior to emerge: to be effective, and to claim its rightful place.

We should not seek to blame or ban all that is harmful to Life (even if we could), and it is good to be overt about this. We know whatever is blamed or banned goes into the shadow. Rather, we should seek to bring about a phase of humanity in which most people *want* to act in ways that support wellbeing most of the time. Although we wish we didn't have to, we can find the courage to tolerate *some* pollution, *some* noise, *some* cruelty. As the mainstream is always telling us, that's reality. It's just that these things have got way out of balance, and we need far less of them, and far more soul, if Life is to thrive.

What Kind of Warrior?

I hope this book has encouraged you to stand up with the warriors, and has brought some clarity about what kind of activist you would rather be. There are many forms of activism: not only because there are many cries for help from the world, but also because there are many different flavours of activist. The great writers of our time have strong opinions about what activism should constitute. For example, Charles Eisenstein argues eloquently against going into battle, whereas George Monbiot is an equally persuasive critic of peaceful resistance. Neither is right or wrong. As Mac Macartney says in *The Children's Fire*, it is easy to be discouraged by the opinions of others. (What creative work would you be bringing forward if you had never heard the opinions of others?) Sometimes you may need to do whatever is necessary to remove yourself as far as possible, for as long as possible, from the opinions of others; to reflect deeply on what is true for you, and then find ways of bringing your truth forward into the world.

Some will tell you your activism is only valid if it comes from love rather than fear. But if you're in your first few decades of life, then fear of losing that life may well be more figural for you than your concern for the greater good - and if you have children or grandchildren, fear for them will of course fuel your fire.

Some say it's time to accept the end of human civilisation; others will urge you to keep striving for our species' future, no matter how unlikely such a thing may seem. Some wise and distinguished elders advocate hope; others invoke terror. Some say stay on the path of growth; others say you're fine as you are. You'll be told that you must find courage; and that it's alright to be small. You will be told by some that you should become skilful in all areas of life, and by others that you have a unique gift, that you can know and use if you undertake a vision quest. In fact, you've encountered all of these positions in this book.

Cut through it all. There is no right way of doing activism, and there is no wrong way, either. Know yourself, know your own truth, and sift through all the wisdom on offer. Don't be seduced by the glamour or charisma of big names. Recognise wisdom wherever you find it: from an experienced man, a learned woman, a timid, hesitant sage, a teenage warrior, or a twisted hawthorn on the edge of a mountain pass. Take what speaks to your truth, and leave the rest to those for whom it's meant. And if you don't know your truth yet, that's fine too. Act as wisely and skilfully as you can, as you bring your work into the world. There are challenges to be met, and you have a part to play.

Courage, dear heart

How we respond to life's challenges is important: they shape who and what we (and Life) will become. When faced with significant dilemmas your embodied and instinctual animal self, naturally embedded in the world, knows what to do. When you need courage to stand boldly in your truth before the world you may find it helps to face North (according to Bill Plotkin's *Wild Mind,* that is where leadership qualities reside). You might remember times when you've felt courageous before; you may choose to think of courageous individuals who lead the way in speaking truth to power. Notice how you feel as you call up, or call in, the qualities of courageous leadership: emotionally, and in your body. If you allow it to, the courage of collective beings will arise and inform you.

In C. S. Lewis' Narnia stories, Aslan tells Trembling Warrior Lucy: "Courage, dear heart", just when she needs to hear it. We can all do with an Aslan to breathe warm, strong Lion breath on us when our courage is faltering. Sometimes we can't find that externally, and so it pays to invest some time in visualising and strengthening your own inner Lion whose breath you can feel when courage fails you; when you face aggressive resistance from those unsettled by the threat of disruption to the familiar establishment with its illusion of strength and stability; or to help you recognise and deal with others' projections. Lion breath can rouse you to mindfulness practice when boredom, apathy, or despair begin to suck you down. Lion breath can give you courage to take bold steps.

When Extinction Rebellion came into being, Larch felt called to respond. He took sabbaticals from paid jobs to commit fully to the work.

> "When I was younger, I saved enough to buy a property. I'm able to let rooms, which keeps enough coming in to cover my basic needs and responsibilities. I don't need much money: all the food I eat would have been thrown away, and if I need to, I know I can build my own home. Not being dependent on money frees me to live my purpose: right now, this feels like what I'm going to do with the rest of my life. Not everyone knows what they want to do with their lives, and I feel blessed to have that clarity."

Brian Swimme and Thomas Berry wrote in T*he Universe Story*, in 1994: 'The future will be worked out in the tensions between those committed to the Technozoic, a future of increased exploitation of Earth as a resource, and those committed to the Ecozoic, a new mode of human-Earth relations, one where the wellbeing of the entire Earth community is the primary concern.'

The future is being worked out in those tensions right now, as Chris Packham faces vitriolic attacks from those with land power and wealth for defending wildlife, popular figures such as Jeremy Clarkson attack Greta Thunberg, and the establishment rears up with all its nasty force to discredit and undermine Extinction Rebellion, a movement whose energy and beauty has come as an unexpected and real threat to its exploitative power base. When I was young, there was no debate between the two in the public arena. The Technozoic ruled conclusively, and the Ecozoic was conveniently dismissed as anti-progress. Now that the Ecozoic is flourishing into the mainstream, the Technozoic can't just write it off as luddite or eccentric; it is forced to fight back.

I described in *The Game* how tension between Life and Destruction was rising; now, it has risen. Juuso Jokiniemi believes that the internet has enabled the swift global connection of both positive consciousness and destructive consciousness, unleashing a new level of energy on both sides. There may not be much more time left for this phase of upheaval to play out before it settles into a more steady state. The nature of that state remains not to be seen, *but to be co-created.*

Perhaps in future decades, reluctant activists will be able to step back from the frontline as a new story becomes mainstream. Or perhaps the battle of the future will be between a micro-chipped, symbiant race, and a race of wild rebels. We will all help make the new story: only when it becomes normal to act as if Life mattered can idealists take a rest. That may be never, but we have to act every day as if it will come, and meanwhile be thankful for the victories we achieve. Eighty-seven-year-old Muriel, who campaigned so hard for Equal Opportunities in the sixties, told me she can't believe how much change she's seen in gender equality issues. Change can happen... change does happen.

My good friend tells me she prays every day after her meditation practice. "I pray for loving kindness to myself and all living beings. I don't say it out loud, but I usually use the same form of words. Sometimes I choose variations: words for what's emerged from meditating. For example, I might add the word 'respect', because that seems to cover it all: if we had respect for other humans, the seas and skies, the forests, the land and all the animals, we would be taking care of them." We have been close friends for many years, but I didn't know this. I ask, what is the purpose of her prayers? "Well, the next day I might still go off and feel angry with someone, complain about them, or do something that isn't ecologically wise. But coming back to that every night is like a wish: an aspiration, or an intention, that I think does make a difference. I don't understand why we still have wars. I mean, I know the logic of why we do, but I don't know why we haven't reached a place where we realise there's a better way of doing things. I do have a wish for it to all stop, and for wellbeing for all beings. I have no idea who's listening, but I just know I've put it out there. It's like a wish, but with more intention: it's more meaningful, because after meditating, I'm in that ritual space."

Wanting to acknowledge the source of her daily Buddhist prayer, I googled it in its entirety. The only result I got was this: 'Buy loving-kindness at Amazon: shop our latest deals in books.' Instantly commodified spirituality. You want sanctity? We'll sell it to you. Loving-kindness has its price, and ours is the best. Spend a bit more and we'll even gift-wrap it, so the recipient feels the professional touch of your outsourced love.

Humanity is capable of *much* better. And we know it. A young University counsellor told me, "There's a backlash to all the image management that sprang up with social media and online promotion. There's a rising desire for authenticity: students are cutting through the fake."

And Paul Hoggett, therapist, academic and co-founder of the Climate Psychology Alliance, remembers not only the protest camps about road building in the nineties, but when the threat of nuclear war hung over young people in the sixties. He told me, "Young climate activists I meet today are so much more aware and emotionally literate than young activists were then. They are much more able to support themselves and each other." That's good: their lives will have a pivotal role in the story of humanity.

The Final Hour

Martin Shaw, mythologist, writes that 'the hour is very late, and we cannot dream what is in store for us.' Elder Mac Macartney says that 'we are in the final hour'. And Bill Plotkin writes with conviction that humanity is finally maturing, after a long period of adolescence.

Areas of our planet are already so hot that they can no longer sustain life, and the ocean's feedback loops have already begun the process that will bring swift and immense changes to the world's weather patterns. Biophiles often speak (sometimes rather hopefully) of humans going extinct, and taking everything else with us. Whether we will be extinguished remains to be seen. But we have already sent many, many species into oblivion, and many more last remaining individuals are dying as I write. If we slide over the edge, we will drag more with us than we have already trampled on in order to get there.

You may, on a despairing day, ask yourself: 'If it's all going down the pan, what's the point?' That's akin to saying, why watch a film, or read a good story, if you know it's going to end? Why live at all, if we're going to die? Such an attitude is redolent of French existentialists such as Sartre, and while it is one version of the truth, it is by no means the only version - unless you've watched enough doom TV dramas or drunk enough alcohol for them to wreak their insidious depressive effects, and forgotten that other interpretations are possible.

Besides all the threats to Life such as a deadly virus, or an asteroid strike, which may pounce from their dark caves at any time, eventually the moon will drift away, and the sun's light will fade, and all life on this planet will end. The last is a very long time in the future, but it is the surest. Our reason to live doesn't have to be and indeed can't be forever: it is now. It is the wren nesting in your garden, or the albatross soaring over the ocean; it is that dear person in a distant town or the next room; it is your precious self, whose body and psyche are at this moment performing complex miracles in your service. Fearing the future does not change the fact that all things end. So rather than fear the end, why not delight in as many moments as possible? And who can say what outcomes we are serving, or what new twists the story of Life may take, as we work with intention to bring about the best today possible? The biosphere has accomplished amazing recoveries before, and will again. It is possible that the future (as we know it) will contain humans – but only if enough humans have enough love for Life to co-create that future. As I complete this book in spring 2019, there is a fresh wind blowing around the world, and the tide appears to be turning. Killing the planet is no longer socially acceptable: caring for the planet is becoming the thing to do. Once a tipping point like this is reached, who can say what can be accomplished, and how quickly?

So, let Trembling Warriors continue to open-heartedly serve all that we love so dearly. Let's continue to plant oak trees for future generations, but let's also make each day precious for this generation of all beings. There is every reason to live diligently and joyfully in each moment that we are alive: for ourselves, and for all beings. We are here for all of us.

Bibliography

Aron, Elaine (2014) *The Highly Sensitive Person.* Thorsons.

Asante, M. K. (2008) *It's Bigger than Hip-Hop* St Martin's Press.

Berry, Thomas, and Swimme, Brian (1994) *The Universe Story.* HarperCollins.

Bernstein, Jerome (2015) *Living in the Borderland.* Routledge.

Cain, Susan (2013) *Quiet.* Penguin.

Coombs, Gill (2014) *Hearing our Calling.* Floris.

Coombs, Gill (2016) *The Game.* KDP.

Edney, Glenn (2016) *The Ocean is Alive.* Oceanspirit.

Goodwin, Brian (2007) *Nature's Due.* Floris.

Ghosh, Amitav (2016) *The Great Derangement.* Uni of Chicago Press.

Griffith, David (2000) *Right Man, Right Time.* Ex Libris Press.

Hopkins, Rob (2013) *The Power of Just Doing Stuff.* Green Books.

Jefferies, Richard (1885) *After London.* Cassell & Co.

Jefferies, Richard (1887) *Unequal Agriculture* Fraser Magazine.

Jeffers, Susan (1987) *Feel the Fear and Do It Anyway.* Penguin.

Jung, C. J. (1921) *Psychological Types.* Rascher Verlag.

Lucas, Caroline (2015) *Honourable Friends?* Portobello Books.

Macartney, Mac (2018) *The Children's Fire.* Practical Inspiration.

Macey, J and Johnstone, C (2012) *Active Hope.* New World Library.

Macfayden, Peter (2017) *Flatpack Democracy.* Eco-Logic.

Monbiot, George (2017) *Out of the Wreckage.* Verso.

Moore, Thomas (2012) *Dark Nights of the Soul.* Piatkus.

Oliver, Mary (2016) *Upstream.* Penguin Random House.

Parlett, Malcolm (2015). *Future Sense.* Matador.

Plotkin, Bill (2003) *Soulcraft.* New world Library.

Plotkin, Bill (2008) *Nature and the Human Soul.* New World Library.

Plotkin, Bill (2013) *Wild Mind.* New World Library.

Pollan, Michael (2009) *In Defense of Food.* Penguin.

Popova, Maria. *Brainpickings* www.brainpickings.org

Silberman, Steve. (2015) *Neurotribes.* Mass Marketing Books.

Steinbeck, John (1952) *East of Eden.* Viking.

Whyte, David (2015) *Consolations.* Many Rivers Press.

Printed in Great Britain
by Amazon